Power Thinking for Success

Power
Thinking
for Success

John N. Mangieri
Cathy Collins Block

BROOKLINE BOOKS

ISBN 1-57129-019-2

Library of Congress Cataloging-in-Publication Data
Mangieri, John N.
      Power thinking for success / John N. Mangieri, Cathy Collins Block.
        p.   cm.
      ISBN 1-57129-019-2 (pbk.)
      1. Reasoning (Psychology) 2. Critical thinking. 3. Problem solving. 4. Decision-making. 5. Success–Psychological aspects.
I. Block, Cathy Collins. II. Title.
BF442.B56 1996
153.4'2–dc20   96-11348
                                   CIP

Published by
BROOKLINE BOOKS
P.O. Box 1047 • Cambridge, Massachusetts 02238-1047

To Donna Zinke Cowman, a great thinker,
who daily uses her skills and abilities
to assure justice for all.

Contents

Introduction ix

How to Read This Book xiv

CHAPTER 1
A Foundation for Success: Reasoning 1

Red Light: STOP to Read, Reflect, or Write 2

Yellow Light: CAUTION: Pause to
Think Both Ways Before You Speak 8

Green Light: GO by Concisely, Accurately, and
Precisely Stating The Reasons for Your Judgments 16

To Review 22

CHAPTER 2
A Foundation for Success: Insight 24

Breaking Away From It All 26

Maintaining Positive Spirits 30

Create As Many Flow Experiences As Possible 36

CHAPTER 3
A Foundation for Success: Self-Knowledge 40

Determining Your Present Level of Self-Esteem 42

Identifying Needs, Talents, And Motives 49

Strengthening Your Self-Concept 59

Conclusion 68

Appendix: Explaining the Self-Esteem Questions 68

CHAPTER 4
Power Thinking and Decision Making 72

Reasoning during Decision Making 73

Insight during Decision Making 90

Self-Knowledge during Decision Making 99

Conclusion 110

CHAPTER 5
Power Thinking and Problem Solving 114

Reasoning during Problem Solving 123

Insight during Problem Solving 145

Self-Knowledge during Problem Solving 152

To Review 157

CHAPTER 6
Power Thinking and Personal Change 159

Reasoning during Personal change 167

Insight during Personal Change 172

Self-Knowledge during Personal Change 175

CHAPTER 7
Work-Related Applications 185

Situation 1 (Decision-Making): Stan 186

Situation 2 (Problem Solving): Wallace 189

Situation 3 (Personal Change): Lucinda 191

Appendix: Lucinda 194

CHAPTER 8
Personal Life Applications 195

Situation 1 (Decision-Making): Glen 195

Situation 2 (Problem Solving): Jan 199

Situation 3 (Personal Change): Mortimer 202

CHAPTER 9
Home and Family Applications 205

Situation 1 (Decision-Making): Ted 205

Situation 2 (Problem Solving): Suzanne 209

Situation 3 (Personal Change): You 211

CHAPTER 10
Your Next Step 215

Your Plan of Action.. 219

About the Authors 224

Appendix: Easy-to-Reference Thinking Aids 225

Introduction

This book's purpose is to improve your thinking processes so you can more effectively attain your goals. Most people don't know how to think as powerfully as they might. Of course, they do think every day — but they do not know how to direct their thoughts to the most effective and positive ends. With *Power Thinking for Success*, you can extend the range of your thinking and focus better on your goals.

A First Question: Can Instruction Improve Thinking?

Recently, we conducted a survey involving approximately 100 business and industry leaders. While all the reporting individuals ranked themselves as "excellent" or "above average" in thinking ability, 22% did not believe that people can be taught to think better. Of the 78% who felt schools and corporate training programs could enhance cognitive development, only 3% indicated that thinking development was a part of their corporate training programs. These programs were designed as "basic thinking skill" instruction for new employees, primarily in clerical positions. None had sought out or created training programs to improve the thinking processes of their higher level managers.

Unfortunately, business and industry leaders are not alone in their lack of understanding about improving thinking skills. We also surveyed approximately 125 teachers-in-training and practicing educators. Eighty-two percent (82%) of these persons recognized the importance of thinking more powerfully and, indeed, were willing to teach it. But 75% of these same individuals could not identify *even a single activity* by which to do so.

These two surveys are not isolated occurrences. Over the years, we have held countless conversations with physicians, government officials, lawyers, engineers, nurses, and individuals from other occupations and professions. In each instance, the results were similar.

Quite simply, despite the fact that these people must use their thinking skills every day, most know little about how to manage their thinking skills to make them more effective. They do not know how to increase the potency of their thought at appropriate points so that powerful thinking will create and advance ideas, nor how to stop a course of negative thinking. In this book, we group these understandings and procedures under an umbrella we view collectively as **power thinking.**

Power thinking mobilizes *a comprehensive array of thinking skills* so that, together and separately, they increase the potency of your thinking. These skills are drawn from the ordinary range of reason, insight, and personal talents. **Power thinking** helps you not only to manage your thinking more effectively but also to integrate your emotions — positive *and* negative — into how you think through problems. In particular, we have become impressed with the critical importance of the self-knowledge that enables you to:

1. see when negative thought and behavior patterns are shaping your thinking,
2. anticipate the consequences of negative thoughts early in your reasoning about the problem, and
3. find ways to move from negative orientations to positive resolutions.

Power thinking adds positive momentum to your reasoning and results in unique contributions because the power of *your* individual talents is employed from the beginning to the end of thinking. By the end of this book, you will experience the differences between good thinking and **power thinking**. For example, through use of the strategies in this book, you will understand the wider implications of your decisions before you make them, anticipate the potential responses of others to your solutions, find ways to use others' talents more effectively, and overcome personal and professional limitations more rapidly.

All thinking draws upon three major domains: **reasoning, insight,** and **self-knowledge. Power thinking** engages them all *cooperatively*. This rich combination creates a synergistic effect, engaging the mind's resources more efficiently in the tasks and/or situations being addressed. By increasing your sensitivity to each domain's unique contribution, you can easily become attuned to using them for small, daily decisions and in larger, life-shaping actions.

Becoming a power thinker requires two stages. In the beginning, most people have to consciously remind themselves to call upon **power thinking** skills when difficulties arise. For this reason, we designed **Thinking Aids:** icons to stimulate your recall of the thinking strategies we teach in this book. Although you will not always have time to refer back to this book when using your **power thinking** skills, these **Thinking Aids** are likely to remain in your subconscious. They can trigger the thinking processes they stand for, enabling you to call upon the relevant strategies.

Our book also contains numerous **Thinking Tools.** These activities are designed to guide you in applying and extending the concepts presented. We urge you to complete them diligently, as they will help you to better understand and utilize the principles of **power thinking** in this book.

The second stage of your development occurs through practice. Practice makes the connections between these processes occur more easily, and with practice you consider the alternatives automatically as you construct your approach to the problem. This practice makes for richer interconnectedness and expands your thinking effectiveness by letting you harness the emotions that empower your rational behavior. Without **power thinking,** you will not always be aware of, or have access to, the powerful energy of insight and individual talents. When these *affective* or emotional dimensions of thought are combined with excellent logical reasoning, you will access opportunities of which others are not consciously aware. **Power thinking** teaches you how to capitalize on the ways in which your own identity and personal approach to the thinking process affect decisions, and how to create avenues for others' powerful thinking to be expressed through joint goals. As a result, **power thinking** helps you turn challenges into new beginnings that many can enjoy.

Thinking should not be a mysterious condition. Rather, it can and should be a process which you can *use* to reach sound decisions and which adds powerful positive energy to your actions. We believe not only that powerful thinking can be taught but also that most, if not all, individuals can learn to do it. Our belief is not mere conjecture. Over the years, we have personally taught thinking development to numerous persons and seen some rather remarkable results. You *can* be taught to think better, just as you can gain prowess in public speaking, typing, mathematics, hitting a golf ball, or expanding your vocabulary. To become more proficient in these — or any other endeavor requiring skill — you must be active! You must know the requisites for doing the task well, and then you must practice the processes until you master them and they become automatic. As you will discover, **power thinking** involves accepting new principles and taking simple actions to actualize your thoughts.

We wrote this book to share the fruits of our years of research about thinking that can make your life more productive — and hence, happier and more satisfying. We have three objectives for this book.

- First, we want to help you increase your self-esteem, creativity, problem-solving abilities, and personal productivity. These aims can be attained through learning and using the strategies and tools in this book that have already increased the achievement of numerous adults and youths with whom we have worked.
- Second, we want to increase your professional competence. As we move from the Age of Technology to the Age of Innovation, you will undoubtedly face tougher professional

challenges than ever before, no matter what your chosen field. You will have to invest more thought in decisions which will have long-range ramifications. By reading this book, you will have more skills to make such decisions.

- Third, we want to help you strengthen your reasoning and spontaneous thinking abilities. We are aware that numerous experiences require spontaneous thinking — that is, "thinking on your feet." In these situations, many people react spontaneously with extemporaneous expressions of negative emotions that have damaging effects. With *Power Thinking for Success*, however, you can limit ineffective negative emotional outbursts, understand why things occur, and work within restraints to achieve positive purposes. You will no longer feel that your life is out of control, or dominated by escapism or sensation-seeking.

Our three goals will have been reached when you can more easily initiate positive changes through your actions, expand your creativity and resourcefulness in thinking about the matters that come before you, produce more successful outcomes for yourself and others, and maintain more satisfying and long-lasting relationships.

We would now like to introduce ourselves as authors. Both of us have taught, published, researched, and administered programs in teaching and learning for 24 years. During this time, we have published more than 100 articles and 12 books between us, including *Teaching Thinking: An Agenda for The Twenty-first Century*; *Creating Powerful Thinking for Teachers And Students*; and *Reason to Read: Thinking Strategies for Life through Literature*. During the last 7 years, we have conducted research and explored the work of cognitive scientists, psychologists, and professors concerning thinking development, which became the foundation for this book. Thus, the thinking strategies presented in this book have emerged from a wide array of disciplines. They are well grounded in research — not only our own, but also that of many others.

HOW TO READ THIS BOOK

As you read, you will be introduced to 25 **Thinking Aids** — graphics that help remind you of the strategies described in *Power Thinking for Success*. These **Thinking Aids** also appear on notecards at the end of the book so that you can cut them out and refer to them after your first reading. Place them in prominent spots in your work area, so they can catch your eye frequently and serve as constant reminders of the strategies.

To master these strategies, you do not have to memorize them or take detailed notes while you read. Instead, we recommend that you read one chapter at a time, pausing frequently to reflect upon its ideas and how you might apply them. This method allows you to organize the information in the ways that best complement your thinking style, talents, and personality. It is also important to know that because your strengths and talents are unique, you will use some thinking strategies more often than others.

We suggest that you read *Power Thinking for Success* in one of two ways. First, you can read with a specific goal in mind, such as to learn a strategy that will solve an immediate problem you face. If you read with a specific objective in mind, you can read that chapter first and use the aid that you prefer to realize its benefits. Then, when you are ready, you can return to select other chapters and strategies concerning a different aspect of your life.

Alternatively, you can read with a less specific objective and proceed consecutively through the chapters. Once you have read through the book, you can select a strategy you want to work on. Then you should practice it intensively for one week. You can cut out the **Thinking Aid** notecard for that strategy and display it in a prominent place (on your desk, on your computer monitor, on your wall or bulletin board) so you can refer to it easily. These reminders will assist your subconscious to integrate these strategies into a permanent, active thinking repertoire.

Reasoning, insight, and self-knowledge form the foundation of powerful thinking. Each is discussed at length in Chapters 1 through 3. By understanding them individually and then collectively, their applications in strategies presented in subsequent chapters will be easier to comprehend.

At the beginning of each chapter, we present a graphic to show you what major ingredients of thinking you have learned by that chapter, adding a section for the topic discussed in the chapter. Its three sections represent reasoning, insight, and self-knowledge. Under each section, strategies that develop powerful thinking are listed for instant reference. These lists serve as a summary of the discussion in each chapter.

Chapters 4 through 6 discuss these three foundation elements with respect to improving your **decision making** (Chapter 4), your **problem solving** (Chapter 5), and your ability to consider and implement **personal change** (Chapter 6). Each of these topics is depicted as a pillar atop the foundation.

Chapters 7, 8, and 9 give you opportunities to see the things you have learned portrayed in actual life situations. Throughout the last seven years, we have found that you learn **power thinking** more rapidly when you read about real-life examples in which **power thinking** was used. Real-life applications allow you to see how the strategies and thinking processes apply to your life, and the ways in which you can use them. Chapter 7 is devoted to professional situations, using examples which you have probably faced in your work life. Chapters 8 and 9 present typical challenges in your personal and family life. In all three of these chapter, you can test your thinking against the **power thinking** of others who applied the tools from Chapters 1 through 6 to change these situations into **power thinking** opportunities.

Chapter 10, entitled "Your Next Step," gives you the opportunity to design a personal plan of action for applying the tools of **power thinking** to current weak points in your own personal and professional thinking processes. We hope you will, at that point, choose ways to incorporate what you have learned into your own thinking habits. The graphic representing this aspect of the thinking process will be a triangle affixed on top of the six pillars to symbolize the roof *you personally place* on these pillars of **power thinking**.

Throughout this book, we will help you to learn by periodically requesting written responses to questions. When we ask you to pause and write your thoughts, you may be tempted not to bother. *We encourage you to overcome this temptation.* Adults who wrote answers in the field-test versions of this book reported that they used the thinking strategies more easily, had a greater understanding of each one, and later understood how several strategies interrelated to advance their problem-solving abilities. *Writing your responses is not a waste of time!* By taking a minute to compose your responses as you read, you can increase your thinking power with the first reading. By responding with your personal thoughts, you make the discussion relevant to *you* personally, which helps you internalize the concepts.

The following questions represent the type of personalized responses we ask of you throughout *Power Thinking for Success*. By answering these two questions, you will set your goal for reading this book. Thereafter, as you read, your subconscious mind will continue to work toward this goal.

✍ Describe as specifically as possible what attracted you to *Power Thinking for Success*, and discuss briefly what you want it to help you accomplish at this point in your life.

_____

_____

_____

_____

_____

_____

✍ Now *set a goal*. For example, what new capability do you want to develop, or what problem do you want to overcome?

_____

_____

_____

_____

At the end of the book, we will return and examine what you just wrote.

Now we begin a journey to develop your **power thinking**. It can be an immensely fruitful journey, but it will not be an easy one. You may need to work your way through this book several times before the processes make complete sense to you. This feeling does not mean that our lessons are unsound, or that you are unable to acquire the skills. With diligence and practice, you will internalize the nuances of the steps. Eventually they will converge into a natural and more automatic script for your style. Even after you reach that level of proficiency, you should still revisit the book occasionally — for reference on a particular step, as a general refresher, or to add new elements of **power thinking** to your repertoire.

Remember — this is your book, so write as many personal thoughts in it as you wish. As you read, we encourage you to answer our questions, highlight sentences that are important to you, and write your insights and comments in the margins.

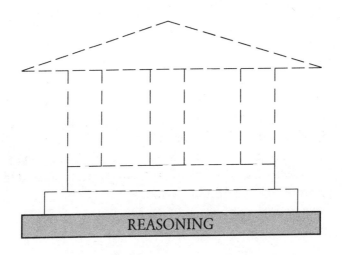

REASONING

CHAPTER 1
A Foundation for Success: Reasoning

Before constructing a house, you must build a foundation to support the structure. For **power thinking** to occur, you must master certain elements of thinking that serve as a foundation — the underpinning of *how* you go about thinking. In this chapter, we discuss *reasoning*, the first of three foundation elements vital to developing thinking power. The others — *insight* and *self-knowledge*, discussed in the following chapters — are used in tandem in **power thinking**. Thus, for you to think powerfully, it is essential that you use strategies to develop all these elements of thinking. We will begin with your reasoning powers.

Reasoning, located in your conscious mind, is the mind's way of taking thought-filled actions. In this section, we describe strategies that will help strengthen your reasoning ability. With them, you will have the tools to:

a. make reasoned decisions and move beyond merely mimicking what you have read or heard;
b. distinguish among *facts*, *opinions*, and *reasoned judgments*;
c. examine issues without promoting your preconceived ideas;
d. minimize miscommunication;
e. listen actively; and
f. speak effectively.

For **Thinking Aid 1** (on the facing page), we have selected the symbol of a traffic light to represent reasoning. We use this graphic so that in the future, traffic lights can remind you of the three sets of powerful reasoning strategies in this chapter. The *red light* symbolizes strategies that assist you to **STOP TO REFLECT** and increase your proactive thinking. The *yellow light* **CAUTION**s you to "think both ways," examining the positives and negatives of all the information at your command before choosing options. The *green light* represents **GO** strategies to "take the right of way" effectively by powerfully stating the reasons for the judgments that you made.

RED LIGHT
STOP to Read, Reflect, or Write

First, we will describe the strategies that enable you to **STOP: Reflecting, Reading,** and **'Riting to Reason.** In essence, you should consciously **STOP** to reason when

1. something doesn't feel right,
2. you have not yet verified new information, or
3. you feel uncomfortable with the direction your thoughts are taking.

THINKING AID 1
REASONING

STOP

Don't just agree or disagree. Think about plusses (+) and minuses (−) involved. Remember that feelings affect my reasoning.

CAUTION

List and think about the facts on both sides of the issue.

GO

State my decision and explanations of how I feel and/or what I think.

STOPping to read, reflect and/or write lets you move beyond an *immediate reaction* and become objective. You will not simply agree or disagree with, but *reason* about new information and others' points of view. The reasoning strategies that enable you to do this are:

- Granting yourself permission to move beyond merely agreeing or disagreeing with others.
- Looking up and away from your work and asking: "What do I *really* want to say/do?"
- Always collecting more information than is presently "on the table" before you take a position.
- Taking notes effectively — both during the initial situation, and as you formulate your response.

☞ *Grant yourself the permission* to do more than agree or disagree with others. When you do this, many dimensions of powerful thinking occur. First, your response to ideas changes. Instead of merely *reacting* to them, you will first consider the validity and value of your preferences, biases, and facts from past (and often outdated) experiences. This pondering limits the subsequent negative effects of voicing your immediate "gut-reaction" support or rejection of ideas. We encourage you to promise yourself that you will think about the pros and cons, and use new information you have gathered, *before* you voice your response — thereby increasing your *proactive thinking*.

Proactive thinking is defined as thinking in advance of acting, so you can anticipate the positive course your words can create in a situation. It allows you to change and prepare the situation in advance. Reflecting before you speak makes your actions more powerful. When you *"proact,"* you ignite thought processes first, and delay your response until you have a considered position. Your actions with others are then more solidly based. Such forethought also places the momentum generated by subsequent actions more directly under your control.

Alternatively, when you *react*, you are placed immediately in the middle of a situation you have not thought through. A good analogy is a game of chess. Beginning players *react* to their opponent's most recent move by taking whatever action strikes them as immediately beneficial. By contrast, champion players think several moves ahead — mentally playing out each possible course of action and their opponent's probable responses, to see what course of action will ultimately prove strongest. This is the essence of proactive reasoning.

In summary: STOPping to reason and challenge your first thoughts about an issue allows you to do more than merely agree or disagree with what exists. It provides time for you to read more about the issue, reflect to develop a sense of the issues, become proactive, and write down the pros and cons of possible positions until a positive course of action emerges.

☞ *Look up and away.* One way to help yourself **STOP** is to pause momentarily and *look up and away* from your work. Ask yourself questions such as "What do I really want to say?" or "What do I really think or believe about this?" Using this process will call upon your unique talents and enable you to think and reason more deeply.

☞ *Take notes effectively as you listen.* This is a very important tool that will help you reason through to a position. Effective notetaking is not a crutch for a poor memory but a tool employed by the *most successful* people in society. To illustrate, notice people's notetaking styles in the next meeting you attend. Some will feverishly scribble everything people say; others will write nothing; and a few will periodically make a note about important issues and their own insights about these issues. The ones in the latter group are the most powerful thinkers. When you take notes:

• Spend the most time writing *your own* thoughts and ideas about the subject, not what others say.

- Outline key points before you comment.
- Do not summarize others' points, but *your own* ideas and thoughts about what you are hearing.

In addition, you will increase your **power thinking** by acting upon your mind's impulses to "jot this idea down." This mental prompt is your conscious mind's request for a concrete reminder, a place-holder for your thought process. It allows you to retain your thoughts about larger issues without being forced to waste energy remembering a specific detail. By taking notes, your conscious mind can spend more time focusing on the *application of your ideas* and *integrating larger principles* effectively so a proactive, original idea can take shape more rapidly.

Similarly, when you need to talk to someone but are unable to do so, jot a note and store it in a place where you can refer to it when you do get to talk with him or her. This proactive step lets you think ahead, so you do not waste an opportunity to exercise and strengthen your own — and others' — **power thinking**. Notes, properly placed, relieve your reasoning mind from having to hold a variety of instructions in active memory until the time when each can be implemented. Carrying such long-term burdens limits your mind's ability to consider new information in the meantime. The following example illustrates the multiple benefits of this single practice; it demonstrates the cumulative impact that these reasoning strategies can have to produce more powerful results in your life.

Example: Cathy teaches courses in the School of Education. One of her graduate students, Suzanne, asked to stay after class one night. She wanted advice about her career. While listening, Cathy jotted down her responses to issues that Suzanne raised, so that she would not have to interrupt. During the half-hour discussion, Suzanne presented three dilemmas. Because Cathy was noting her own ideas, she could concentrate completely upon Suzanne's ideas *until Suzanne had finished*, without forgetting the points that she wanted to make about each. Also, because "taking notes" suspended Cathy's impulse to make judgments, Suzanne could describe all the points on her mind without being misdirected or misinterpreted.

The next morning Cathy had another idea. Because she wouldn't see Suzanne for a week, she jotted this idea on a note and placed it as the first paper on her materials for class. This action enabled Cathy to complete, a week later, a proactive communication that proved helpful to Suzanne, without burdening Cathy's mind with having to remember it.

Without this **power thinking** strategy, Cathy would have forgotten her idea; then, as Cathy watched Suzanne continue to pursue less effective career options, she might even have lost confidence in her abilities to counsel students, decreased her trust in her own insights, and perceived invalid limitations to her talent of assisting others. Thus, what appears to be a simple, rational strategy — to **STOP**, write down an idea, and place it in a location where it will serve as a reminder at the appropriate time — turns out to be a powerful proactive behavior that advances both Suzanne's and Cathy's future contributions to others. This is a single example of the power of the strategies we present in this book.

In summary: **STOP**ping to read, reflect, and write, and granting yourself permission to do more than merely agree or disagree with others, are the first steps toward **power thinking**. Each time you begin to think, remember to grant yourself permission to move beyond merely agreeing or disagreeing with others, and develop your considered position by:

- Looking up and away from your work to ignite insight,

- Collecting more information than is currently "on the table" before you take a position, and

- Taking notes effectively, both during the initial presentation and to formulate your best response.

✍ To implement these strategies, pause now for a moment. On the next line, write the action you want to take to **STOP** more effectively in the future.

_____

✍ Which of the strategies in this section of the book do you most need to practice? Reflect for a moment about when you can likely employ this strategy — and the others — in your immediate future.

_____

_____

YELLOW LIGHT

CAUTION: Pause to Think Both Ways Before You Speak

The **CAUTION** stage is the second set of strategies we propose for more powerful reasoning. These strategies enable you to **CAUTIOUS**ly find inconsistencies in facts, opinions, and judgments before moving forward, to consciously and effectively **Think Both Ways Before You Speak**. They are to:

- Listen carefully.
- Rephrase others' comments using their own words.
- Read body language.
- Traverse new territory from many directions.
- Ask questions.

These strategies lead power thinkers to greater success. For example, by listening carefully _to every person_, power thinkers produce the following benefits:

- hard feelings don't develop that have to be mended later;
- bridges aren't burned which have to be rebuilt;
- time is not wasted in retracing steps unnecessarily; and
- prior miscommunications do not weigh on their minds, so their full attention can be engaged in the situation of the moment.

☞ *Listen carefully.* Power thinkers listen attentively even to people they don't like. By *actively* listening to every person, you become more attentive. For instance, you may be a person who enjoys attacking problems. When "complainers" come to talk, you do not want to listen because you have difficulty sympathizing with them. You may say to yourself, "Stop whining and feeling sorry for yourself. Get busy correcting the situation!" However, if you remember the **CAUTION** step in reasoning and "think both ways before you speak," you can gain helpful insights into opposite sides of an issue and increase your ability to receive information objectively. Moreover, many people do not reveal the depth of their perspective until the end of their comments. If you do not listen attentively, you will not hear as many ideas because people will not bring theirs to you.

☞ *Rephrase others' comments using their own words.* How can you "hold on" to other people's words and keep an active mind while listening? Pay attention to the exact words people say, then use their words in your replies. This action increases attentiveness and assures people that you are really listening and that they have been *heard and understood.*

Example: John seeks to understand exactly what people say. One day we were discussing Cathy's sister-in-law and John asked what she was like. Cathy said, "She is such a very nice person." John responded: "I would have thought so." Cathy asked, "Why?" He replied: "Because an accurate description of your husband would include the words *very nice*." By using the same words

Cathy had used, John communicated that he not only had heard and understood her, but agreed with what she had said.

We encourage you to practice this strategy the next time someone talks to you. Repeat the words they use and notice the results.

☞ *Read body language.* The next **CAUTION** strategy is to ask about the information you receive through *body language, non-verbal communications, and mannerisms.* Non-verbal information can cause misinterpretation due to mixed messages: a conflict between someone's verbal communication (what they say) and the information contained in their body language. When people's verbal and non-verbal messages contradict each other, or confuse you, say: "I'm confused. You said ＿＿＿＿ but seem to mean ＿＿＿＿. Am I correct?" If you don't ask this question, you are forced to choose whether to base your actions on the verbal *or* the non-verbal information. In such situations, you will have only a 50/50 chance of responding correctly to the person's intended message.

To practice asking this question: Think of a person whose actions confused you recently. Suppose you had then asked that person: "I'm confused. You said ＿＿＿＿ but seem to mean ＿＿＿＿. Am I correct?" Would you have learned more about the person or the subject? Would a misunderstanding have been avoided?

The next time a confusion occurs with this person, explain the conflicting messages you are receiving, and ask these questions. The subsequent explanation will enable you to respond more directly to his or her true intent.

☞ *Traverse the territory from many directions.* The third strategy requires you first to *identify your preconceived viewpoints about a topic* early in the **power thinking** process. When you are aware of your predispositions, you will not attempt to convince others (or yourself) that they are objectively reasoned judgments. Without this **CAUTION** step to gain self-knowledge, you may act upon biases rather than facts. Once you have this self-knowledge, you can begin to make a conscious effort to examine the issue from many different perspectives. We call this *traversing the territory from many directions.*

Our research indicates that most powerful thinkers have developed methods for doing this. While it may sound like a simple and common-sense ability, it cannot be achieved without practicing ways to proactively challenge your own bias. To make this reasoning process automatic, we suggest the following exercise.

Draw a circle and label the center with the name of the issue you are working to understand. On the perimeter of the circle, write the names of the people or conditions affected by the issue. Draw a line from each person or condition to the central issue, and write on it the primary link between them. When all the links are completed, you can visually discern the factors involved in the issue and understand *why* one path of information is more attractive to you than others. An illustration, using the following example, appears in **Figure 1-1** on the next page.

Example: Cost-cutting has become a crucial issue for many of our nation's businesses. The president of one company, a friend whom we'll call Milt, is very adept at cost-cutting and makes it a high priority in his business decisions. In fact, he has a tendency to make it his *highest* priority.

Milt must not only become aware of his preconceived view of the importance of cost containment, but also closely examine its effect upon his actions. For example, a subordinate, Kevin, may approach him with a new initiative that would require a capital outlay of $100,000. Milt's usual inclination is to reject such an "expensive" request out of hand. This action would be appropriate if the proposal is frivolous. However, if the idea has the real potential to yield a mil-

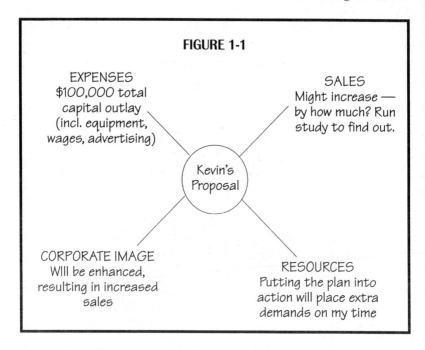

FIGURE 1-1

EXPENSES
$100,000 total
capital outlay
(incl. equipment,
wages, advertising)

SALES
Might increase —
by how much? Run
study to find out.

Kevin's
Proposal

CORPORATE IMAGE
WIll be enhanced,
resulting in increased
sales

RESOURCES
Putting the plan into
action will place extra
demands on my time

lion-dollar profit, then Milt's biased predisposition will have seriously restricted the success of his business.

Are we asking Milt to abandon his views on cost containment? No! Rather, we believe that he must recognize them and make a conscious effort to *traverse the territory* by examining in an objective manner those ideas that conflict with his preconceived inclination. With regard to Kevin's proposal, he might draw the diagram in Figure 1-1.

☞ *Ask questions.* In the words of American philosopher Anthony Jay, "The uncreative mind can spot wrong answers, but it takes a creative mind to spot wrong questions." Use **Thinking Aid 2** to remind you of this principle.

Before asking a question, check the reasons for asking it. *Is the question an attempt to understand others or to reach truth rather than to push your own ideas?* If it is, people will sense your collaborative intent and engage in freer, more honest exchanges. By considering in advance how your questions can

THINKING AID 2
ASK QUESTIONS TO CLARIFY

condition and change the environment to achieve a more positive purpose, you can ensure that your inquiries will not be self-centered and self-serving. Moreover, your questions will increase people's trust in you. With increased trust, you will receive additional, valuable information on which to base subsequent actions. Taking the extra time to ask questions increases the likelihood that you will discover potential difficulties before you reach a decision.

Example: A very successful man frequently asks this question of people who bring him problems: "I sincerely want to know how your experience can assist our company not to make this mistake again. What do you think we can do to avoid this difficulty in the future?"

Equally important, because you ask questions, people will not spend time trying to convince you that their beliefs are factual. They know *you* will ask questions like "Why?" or "How do you know?" if they try to clothe opinion as fact. Because they know you will ask them for verification, they will talk more objectively.

You can also use questioning to encourage more powerful thinking in meetings. Test this principle: The more powerful questions you ask in a group, the more successful the group's work becomes. The more negative statements — and questions that do not reflect powerful thinking — presented in a meeting, the less effective that meeting will be. **Thinking Tool A** (on the facing page) lists questions used by highly successful people to elicit powerful thinking in groups.

It is also important to understand *why* asking questions is so difficult. Many people do not like to have questions asked of them because they think some questions are designed to dissuade them from their beliefs. Generally, people do not want their beliefs to be altered by others, regardless of whether their beliefs are correct. Therefore, when questioned, many people become defensive very quickly. Moreover, people tend to fear questions that they cannot answer with facts or rea-

THINKING TOOL A

POWERFUL QUESTIONS

1. Why?

2. Is the most important point _____ or _____?

3. What do you mean by _____?

4. If I understand you correctly, you mean _____. Is that correct?

5. Where will the point you are making *not* apply? How does _____ relate to _____?

6. If your idea is accepted, what is the greatest change that will occur?

7. Would you say more about _____?

8. What is the difference between _____ and _____?

9. Would _____ be an example?

10. Is it possible that _____? What else could we do?

11. If _____ happened, what would be the result?

soned judgments.

If you fear questioning or being questioned, use the previously described **CAUTION** strategies to ensure the accuracy of your answers before you speak. Checking the accuracy of your claims will build your confidence; you will no longer fear asking the "wrong" or *tough* question. Instead, you will ask questions like those on **Thinking Tool A** to avoid rhetoric and uncover important issues more rapidly.

A strategy for employing powerful "tough questions" is to end discussions and meetings by asking: "What question *should* I (we) have asked that I (we) didn't?" When you ask this question, you stimulate an integrative review of the thinking that occurred during the meeting — and you identify where **power thinking** might take you during the next one, focusing the participants on thinking proactively for the next meeting. This proactive focus will help other important issues emerge.

In summary: Your reasoning ability increases in direct pro-
                 portion to the number of **CAUTION**s you
                 engage, partly because you become more con-
                 fident of the most powerful way to proceed.
                 In this second stage of reasoning, we encour-
                 age you to "think both ways" by considering
                 the same issue from as many perspectives as
                 possible, and by asking lots of questions.

GREEN LIGHT

GO by Concisely, Accurately, and Precisely Stating The Reasons for Your Judgments

The third set of **power thinking** strategies involves *speaking*. Having stopped to think through your position, present it *C*oncisely, *A*ccurately, and *P*recisely (CAP).

- *Concise* speech eliminates irrelevant details.
- *Accurate* speech avoids misleading statements, verifies facts, and remains silent unless the speaker is one hundred per-

cent sure that the information is valid or the opinion is honest.

- *Precise* speech eliminates overgeneralizations, exaggerations, and unwarranted superlatives.

To remember these three characteristics of powerful speech, envision your language as a *CAP* that will protect you from the unnecessary "rain and hail" of untrustworthiness. When your language is **CAP**ped, you gain the reputation of providing specific, valid, and thought-filled information which builds others' trust in your words. The strategies you can use to **CAP** your speech are:

- Making your statements productive, not self-defensive.
- Having your point clear in your mind before you speak.
- Learning to "assert, illustrate, then stop."
- Using specific, concrete nouns and exact verbs.
- Avoiding generalizations.
- Not prefacing comments with disclaimers.

☞ *Make your statements productive, not self-defensive.* To **CAP** your speech, avoid entering meetings with the main objective of championing only your own opinion throughout the meeting. Speak to move productively ahead toward a collective solution, rather than to fulfill your need to be right. By speaking *C*oncisely, *A*ccurately, and *P*recisely, you will be less likely to speak *only* to convince others to join your *preconceived position*. Instead, enter with the intent of:

- identifying how individual comments change your preconceived position and the direction of thought about an issue, and
- using **STOP** and **CAUTION** strategies every time before you speak.

   Every one of your comments should elicit subsequent comments from others that either halt or advance the direction you establish. Without such careful examination, your comments could be wrong, or they might be right for the wrong reasons.

If arbitrariness or apathy exists within a group, or if some-one pleads for acceptance of their perspective above the greater good, use **CAP**ped speech to call upon people's sense of fair-ness and impartiality.

Example: Imagine an instance involving group hiring decisions. One member wants to hire a specific person and pleads that person's case from a biased position. You can call upon the group's sense of impartiality by saying: "If we want to add another member to our team who has strengths in areas in which we are already strong, we will choose one candidate; if we want our unit to move in new directions, we will choose another. Our intention is to do what is best for our team."

☞ *Have your point clear in your mind before you speak.* With **CAP**ped speech, your mind acts before your mouth begins. Before you speak, answer (perhaps in your notes to yourself) the following questions: "What is *the point* I want to make? How can I best phrase this point to move us forward?" If you cannot discern the answers clearly before you speak, your mind has not completed its work. These statements prioritize your thoughts and point them, proactively, in the direction you desire. It is crucial to determine in advance the effect you want your words to achieve, because the moment you begin to speak, listeners mentally classify your message for either attention or dismissal. This principle ties in to the next strat-egy for **CAP**ping your speech.

☞ *Assert, illustrate, then stop.* Based on your choice of words, listeners instantly form an opinion about how important your message is. **CAP**ped, effective speaking makes your statements stand out. To discover what is simple and act upon it is an exceedingly challenging task, but one you can accomplish. (Lawyers, for instance, are trained to give powerful closing statements that do not exceed a few succinct sentences.) To convey your intent skillfully, the first step is telling people what you know and what you intend in approximately two sentences. Formulate a statement that portrays *your message and intent accurately, specifically and precisely.* Do not overstate your case or say more than you know. Follow this statement with an illustrative fact, summary statement, or example of that image in action, rather than trying to restate your intention through many, more general descriptive sentences. Express your main message in one sentence, use a second to support it, *then stop.*

Example: If you *feel* that an action is imperative and have determined that two points comprise your main message, say: "Taking an action on _____ is essential. Without it, _____ will reoccur."

Without **CAP**ped speech, you will convey a less powerful message through statements such as, *"I think we might want to think about _____. It's really kind of important, you know?"*

Then *stop talking.* If people want to know more, they will ask. Waiting for their response before you say any more is the second step.

☞ *Use specific, concrete nouns and exact verbs.* Taking the time to say specifically what you mean eliminates miscommunication. Choose more picturable, visual nouns and vivid verbs.

Example: Instead of simply telling an employee to write a three-page summary report, ask for a three-page report in the format you have shown in a sample. Add that it should end with a persuasive two-paragraph conclusion, and that the final sentence of the report should specify the actions the readers should take.

☞ *Avoid generalizations.* If you constantly use superlatives like *best, most, all, never,* and *always,* people will judge you to be irrationally extreme, or a weak thinker who does not value precision. To avoid this impression, continue to use **STOP** and **CAUTION** thinking until a vivid example or specific point can be expressed *C*oncisely, *A*ccurately, and *P*recisely [**CAP**].

This strategy means that you will leave many meetings having said less than others. In fact, you frequently will not express your exact thoughts during the hour's meeting time, since you were **STOP**ping to reflect and write and **CAUTION**-ing by reconsidering options from many perspectives. *This will not be a loss, however* — for when you cannot describe an idea specifically, the idea is often too weak or nebulous to share except with trusted mentors and friends. Subsequently, through private discussions with such people, your idea can be shaped into a succinct and powerful example. When this occurs, others can more easily understand and use it to move more rapidly toward a positive purpose.

☞ *Don't preface your comments with disclaimers.* A *disclaimer* is a phrase placed before a main idea statement that gives a reason not to accept or believe the idea that is to follow. Some examples of disclaimers are:

- "This may be a stupid idea, but...";
- "I know it probably won't work, but...";
- "I could be wrong, but...",
- "I've been wrong before, but....";
- "I know I don't have much experience, but...",
- "You may disagree, but...",

Phrases such as these weaken your message: they supply rea-sons why others should not pursue your ideas. They direct listeners to disavow your comments before they have even heard them. Disclaimers immediately encourage listeners to search for reasons to disagree with you. After all, you began by asserting that "You may disagree..." — indicating that argu-ments already exist that oppose your position — so your lis-teners will help you find them! Similarly, if you state that your idea could be wrong, many listeners hastily invent rea-sons why it *is* wrong, if only to help you "save face."

To keep disclaimers from creating this near-instantaneous mental response, state your idea directly, without an opening phrase. Alternatively, if you feel the need to preface your re-marks, use preludes that are positive. For example, instead of saying "I haven't had much experience, so I may be wrong," say "From my fresh perspective, I see these benefits: ...."

Disclaimers often occur when people do not have the courage to support the ideas they are about to express. You can eliminate disclaimers by **STOP**ping to clarify to yourself the intent of your message, and allowing time to mount your courage. Other people use disclaimers to communicate their sensitivity to positions that others hold. Unfortunately, the use of disclaimers to achieve this goal is counterproductive because it erroneously conveys that you are a weak or rash, rather than a powerful, thinker.

Besides monitoring your own speech for disclaimers and other un**CAP**ped patterns, you can analyze people's responses to your comments to detect if you are projecting weakness. For example: when in meetings, if others remove their eye contact or rarely act upon your suggestions, you are not speaking *C*oncisely, *A*ccurately, and *P*recisely. If this occurs, re-read these sections to review the strategies we have discussed. Another effective strategy to avoid projecting weakness is to behave as if you already feel self-confident. Become a "front-row person"; make eye contact even in the hallways; walk with your head high and with a purposeful gait; project a positive smile when you interact with others.

These speaking strategies and actions develop your ability to communicate positively and effectively, even with those who hold opposite positions. As Napoleon said, "The people to fear are not those who disagree with you, but those who disagree with you and are too cowardly to let you know."

In summary: The third set of powerful reasoning strategies is to use *C*oncise, *A*ccurate and *P*recise (**CAP**ped) speech. You can do so by:

- speaking to move positive collective solutions ahead productively, rather than to persuade others that your perspective is correct;

- using specific, concrete nouns and verbs; and

- not prefacing comments with disclaimers.

TO REVIEW

✍ What are the three sets of strategies in powerful reasoning that create a foundation for powerful thinking? Write below, in your own words, the strategies you have learned. You may look back in the chapter to help you remember and review them.

1. _____

2. _____

3. _____

In closing, have you determined which of these sets of strategies you would most like to implement for yourself? If not, a method you can use to make this decision is to recall statements others have said to you. If someone has made one of the following statements about your reasoning in the past, we recommend that you reread the pages of this chapter that we indicate after that statement. Doing so enables you to select the most specific action you can take to strengthen your personal reasoning abilities.

1. If others say that you frequently make snap judgments, you would probably profit from practice in **STOP**ping: to read and reflect, to take notes correctly, and to give yourself permission not to merely agree or disagree with others.

✍ Which of the strategies in the discussion on pages 2–8 do you want to practice first?

_____

2. If others say that you "never listen," you may need to develop more **CAUTION** strategies to *think both ways* as you reason. By asking more questions, attending to non-verbal language, and traversing issues from many perspectives, you will increase the power of your reasoning.

✍ Which of the strategies in the discussion on pages 8–15 do you want to practice first?

_____

3. If others say that you are stubborn, you may often act on your first line of reasoning without considering other possibilities. If you agree that you do not consider as many possibilities as you would like, you can **CAUTIOUS**ly examine the positive and negative implications of new information and draw graphs of reasoning links in order to traverse ideas from many perspectives.

✍ Which of the strategies in the discussion on pages 8–15 do you want to practice first?

_____ .

4. If your reasons are frequently refuted by others, you would profit from developing more methods of **GO**ing ahead by speaking *C*oncisely, *A*ccurately, and *P*recisely.

✍ Which of the strategies in the discussion on pages 16–22 do you want to practice first?

_____

5. If others do not frequently seek out your ideas, you would profit from GIVING REASONS FOR YOUR IDEAS by speaking *C*oncisely, *A*ccurately, and *P*recisely. For example, have you planned the intent of your message before you speak? Have you eliminated disclaimers and generalizations?

✍ Which of the strategies in the discussion on pages 16–22 do you want to practice first?

_____

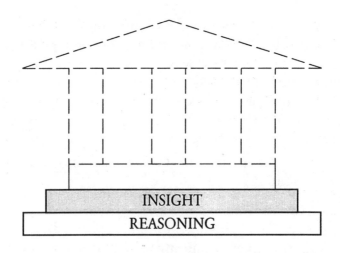

INSIGHT

REASONING

CHAPTER 2
A Foundation for Success: Insight

Reality can be divided into two spheres: the *external* world of objects, actions, and reasons, and the *internal* world of insights, visions, and feelings about these reasonings, objectives, and events. The purpose of Chapter 1 was to increase the power of your conscious reasoning in terms of the external world.

Chapter 2 is designed to increase your access to your *internal* world and, thus, the power and saliency of your subconscious insight in your thinking. *Insight* is the ability to immediately know without conscious reasoning. Daniel Isenberg of the Harvard Business School described it this way:

Insight is not the opposite of rationality; nor is it a random process of responding and guessing. Rather, it is the total of extensive experience with "yourself-in-implementation," and lessons of experience, which are well-founded and important elements in success.*

An interesting value of insight is that there are truths that reason cannot attain. Because the subconscious organizes information in unanticipated ways, the ideas and truths derived from intuition can be broader and more acute than those constructed by the rational mind. Through the inspiration, spiritual understandings, and feelings that insight adds, powerful thinkers can often "feel that something is right" before they can explain it.

Example: You can probably recall occasions when "something told you" not to bother doing a task — such as running a particular errand that day — so you held off. Later, you remembered that the place you needed to go for that errand was closed that day. Your insight *knew*, even though your conscious reasoning did not take the scheduled closing into account. Because you listened to your insight, you did not waste the time driving and become frustrated.

Equally important is the contribution *emotion* makes to insightful knowledge. Personalized feelings, memories, perceptions, gut reactions, temperament, visualizations, and spirituality dictate that no single answer exists that is correct for everyone. However, through powerful insight, you can be assured that the answer you develop, for yourself, will be totally and completely correct for you. This is true because, as scientists have discovered, insight assists the mind to scan selectively among all the options in your experience. In this search, the subconscious utilizes virtually all of your body, mind, motor, and adjustment systems to assemble the information and help you select the most relevant. This total-

* Isenberg, D. (1993). "Reason Versus Insight." *Harvard Business Review*, vol. 179, p. 10.

being investment increases the probability that the mental and emotional energy you invest will continue to operate until an idea *finally* "clicks" and you can judge its compatibility with your multiple needs. This phenomenon also explains why a correct solution "feels good" and generates your enthusiasm.

Psychologists and physicians have also discovered that when your insight is powerful, the rational mind automatically slows down and limits the number of distractions and messages it will receive. This "stilling of the mind" increases beta brain wave activity and the vividness and clarity of mental images. Therefore, the longer your mind remains in this state, the longer the subconscious can make explicit connections between these images of experiences, memories, perceptions, and imagination, and the greater number of insights you will generate.

Power thinking exists only when insight and reason unite; this union is too priceless a possession to sacrifice by acting on either facts or "gut reactions" alone. The next sections of this chapter describe the strategies that help you develop and mobilize your insights. These strategies also assist you to examine your perceptions, beliefs, emotions, and view of the world so negative misconceptions in your subconscious can be eliminated. Powerful insight, just like powerful reasoning, is based on three sets of strategies: *breaking away from it all, maintaining positive spirits*, and *creating flow experiences*. **Thinking Aid 3** (on the facing page) is designed to remind you of these powerful strategies.

BREAKING AWAY FROM IT ALL

"Breaking away from it all" is very important, especially when worry and negative emotions taint your thinking. Merely avoiding stress and difficulties will not stimulate insight, however. People may have told you that you should "stop and smell the roses along the way," believing that just "taking time out" will revitalize your insight. Unfortunately, we find that most people who "stop to smell the roses" either smell *too many* or *the wrong kind* to become powerful thinkers! If *breaking away* is to ignite insight, it must:

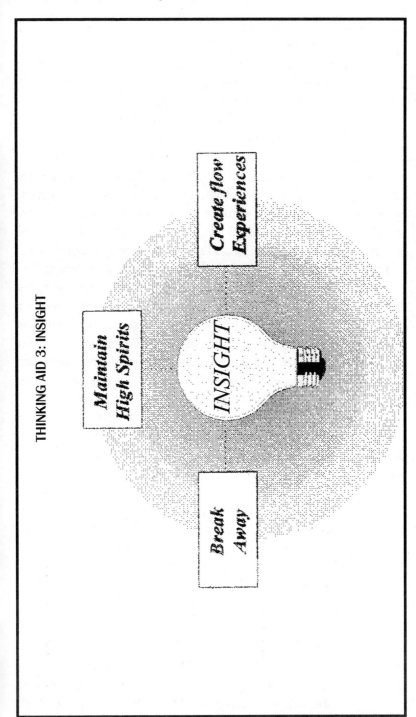

THINKING AID 3: INSIGHT

Create flow Experiences

Maintain High Spirits

INSIGHT

Break Away

- eliminate your fatigue,
- completely clear your mind for a few moments,
- uplift your spirits,
- provide new scenery, sounds, or tactile stimuli, and
- change the blood-flow pattern in your body (e.g., if you have been seated for a long period of time, try standing up or walking to rekindle your insight).

This kind of *breaking away* is particularly important when you become frustrated. Frustration is a sign that you have reached the point where your rational mind, searching laboriously for a solution, has exceeded the limit of its abilities. At such times, physical activities can remove tension and move more oxygen to the brain and muscles, which stimulates beta wave activity and insight.

In our research, we have watched how power thinkers employ *breaking away* effectively. They told us they spend long hours on a single task, executing powerful reasoning strategies to create new solutions. During this period, anguish and frustration often set in. If they persist at that point, mistakes occur frequently and tension mounts. Instead, power thinkers slow down or pause in their work on the task. They move away from the task by *breaking away*, even momentarily, so that all the work that came before integrates with their subconscious visions and feelings — and something clicks. Through this process, insight suddenly moves them toward a powerful new solution with a single great leap.

☞ One type of breaking away is *reverie.* Reverie involves consciously requiring yourself to think of nothing in particular. It can be an extended pause for several minutes, or only a momentary pause — as long as the eyes look away from the task at hand, and the mind recalls pleasant thoughts. Reverie as a component of powerful thinking is being viewed more positively in business: it has proven to invite insight into problem-laden situations.

Example: A manager of one of the Fortune 500 companies was showing a new employee to his office. As they walked, they passed the office of a high-ranking executive who was seated with his feet on the desk, twiddling his thumbs. As they passed, the new employee asked why the company paid this executive so much money "just to do nothing." The manager answered, "You know, last year that man had an idea that earned our company one million dollars. And when the idea occurred to him, he was doing exactly what he is doing now!"

If *breaking away* is difficult for you at first, we recommend that you schedule routine moments to "not think of anything in particular." You need only set aside a few moments each day. Even this limited amount of time can significantly increase the power of your insight.

In summary: *Break-away experiences* increase insight and sub-conscious attention to problem-laden situations. The key is that break-away experiences must accomplish all the physical changes necessary to ignite insight. Because every person's style is different, you must think about the best activities you have used in the past that:

1. completely eliminated *your* fatigue — e.g., physical exercise, deep breathing, taking a shower;

2. completely cleared *your* mind from details of the day — e.g., gardening, knitting, reading;

3. lifted *your* spirits — e.g., music, conversation, dining;

4. provided *you* with the type of new scenery, sounds, or tactile experiences that you enjoy; and

5. changed the blood-flow patterns in *your* body — e.g., lying on a slantboard, receiving a massage, walking around, doing your daily workout.

You must learn which activities you can prof-
itably use for momentary or extended *breaks
away* from projects, and which can be used
weekly to strengthen the power of your insight. These experiences will also lead you to
better engage the second strategy for powerful insight: *maintaining positive spirits.*

MAINTAINING POSITIVE SPIRITS

The second, equally important component is *understanding and
nurturing positive emotions.* When your insight is powerful, you can
spot the nucleus of negative emotions and harness their negative
energy for beneficial purposes. Because emotions and feelings are
subconsciously governed, they are not logical or consistent; they
often defy logical analysis and cannot be justified. Their positive
power strengthens you by being truly *experienced, not explained.*

Because truth, love, peace, hope, and joy are gifts that guide
people through many difficulties, recognizing what *truly* brings
these emotions into *your* life is critical. Manifestations of emotional knowledge — such as character, patience, and integrity — are
built through conscious nurturing of these positive emotions. Such
cultivation requires an appreciation of what a given experience
means — rationally, insightfully, and emotionally — to yourself
and to others. It also includes the ability to see something divine
in every other person.

As you become a power thinker, your emotional level will
dwell more consistently at the top three levels of the emotional
scale (shown in **Thinking Aid 4** on p. 32). We encourage you to
refer frequently to this emotional scale graphic so you can understand your negative and positive feelings. A first step in recognizing and nurturing your positive emotions is to identify, very specifically, what lowers your mood and emotions.

Understanding, Accessing, and Harnessing Your Negative Feelings

The order of the emotional states reflects how close to the surface each emotion lies. Anger is the most assertive negative emotion — and the easiest to elicit, because anger is insight's automatic reaction to whatever interferes with your ability to achieve goals or understanding. Hurt and fear are more difficult to elicit. These emotions usually require that you misinterpret a line of reasoning or insight, or that you repeatedly experience a misunderstanding.

While negative emotional energies can ignite instantly, the higher and more positive energies (satisfaction from assuming responsibility, contentment, enthusiasm and joy) require more time to be felt.

The next discussion explains the emotional scale. The levels of emotion are depicted in **Thinking Aid 4** (on the next page) in order of their importance as components of powerful thinking.

Level 1: Anger. Anger is an emotional energy that cannot be destroyed or forgotten. It has to be converted. Anger is the easiest emotion to display because society has convinced us, especially males, that it is acceptable to express anger, but inappropriate to express hurt or fear. Anger is also easiest to elicit because it is insight's first reaction to something that interferes with your ability to accomplish goals or understanding. If it is not filtered through the reasoning strategies of **STOP, CAUTION**, and **CAP**ped speech, anger can expand to become unjust blame, resentment, envy, jealousy, or hate. In its most advanced forms, anger becomes a permanent emotional state in which negative biases about a specific event or person/people consume your life and contaminate all reasoning and insight about that issue.

The most effective method of moving beyond anger is to reason, write, or reflect to identify what you can do to remove the obstacle to goal achievement or understanding. Such reasonings usually produce an insight about a blind spot in your reasoning processes that you can eliminate.

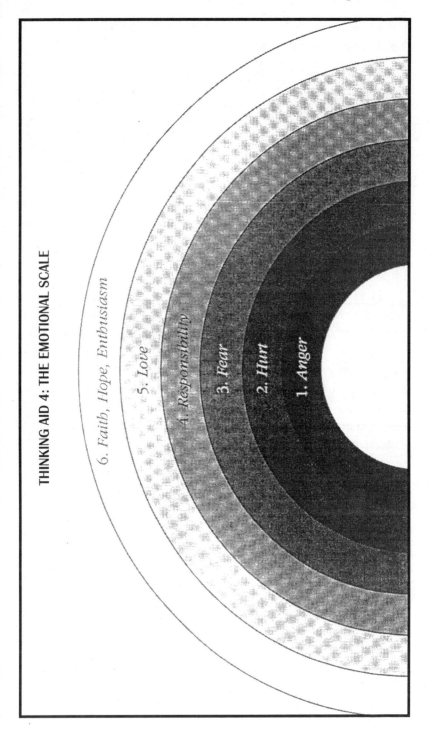

THINKING AID 4: THE EMOTIONAL SCALE

6. *Faith, Hope, Enthusiasm*

5. *Love*

4. *Responsibility*

3. *Fear*

2. *Hurt*

1. *Anger*

Example: A power thinker who becomes angry at incompetent
           actions by an employee writes down the specific inci-
           dent that angered her, writes the possible action paths
           in a circle around it, and writes reasons for pursuing
           each action on links between the incident and the
           potential resolutions. By drawing this graph, the power
           thinker may discover that a weakness in her leader-
           ship style — e.g., a vague mission statement, unclear
           task expectations, an invalid reward structure — cre-
           ated a climate where this type of incompetence would
           be tolerated by lower levels of management.

Level 2: Hurt. Hurt is the second easiest emotion to feel. However, because hurtful feelings are so painful, you may quickly re-
press them through *denial*: that is, pretending you do not feel the
way you do. The most effective method of moving beyond hurt is
to admit your pain to those involved. With this admission, you
move to Level 4 of *positive* emotional energy: the satisfaction which
comes from assuming your responsibility. Without this admission, you may unknowingly intensify your pain until it becomes
self-pity, sadness, disappointment, martyrdom, or depression.

Level 3: Fear. The third easiest emotion to elicit is fear. Fear *can*
be a positive as well as a negative emotion, as it serves to protect
you from harm. Protecting yourself from imaginary dangers, however, can be very detrimental to powerful thinking. Fear of failure
is a good example: The fear can loom so large that you delay
action. Yet it is this delay, not any personal shortcoming, which
often leads to your failure.

Example: No matter what the arena, the anxiety that fear builds
           in anticipation of an event exaggerates fantasies of fail-
           ure and catastrophe. For example, an irrational fear of
           failure in the workplace can occur in this way: "If I
           bring up this new idea," you tell yourself, "and it flops,
           then I'll make a fool of myself at the meeting. My boss
           will see me as incompetent, and pass me by for the

promotion I want."

So you shut up and say nothing. You tell yourself, "Better safe than sorry," curl up and hide in your comfort zone — and, due to your own inaction, never receive the promotion.

Recall how frequently in the past, when you faced whatever you feared, you discovered there was much less to fear than you had imagined. Unchecked irrational fear decreases your positive energy and can manifest itself as paranoia, distrust, selfishness, shock, and detachment from others. Fear is overcome through proaction and **CAP**ped speech.

Transforming anger, hurt and irrational fears into more positive and powerful emotional powers. Kahlil Gibran wrote, "When you are sorrowful, look again in your heart, and you shall see that, in truth, you are weeping for that which has been your delight."

We urge you not to give others control over your emotions.

Example: Instead of saying to someone else, *"You make me so mad,"* realize that when someone else's action stimulates negative emotions in you, it is because that action shook an aspect of your emotional or cognitive thoughts over which you have not yet gained self-control. **Power thinking** means recognizing when a person has activated one of these sensitive aspects of your life. When you make this recognition, use statements that begin with the word "I" instead of the word "you": *"I am angry. I am hurt and wonder if I misinterpreted. I am afraid, and I will _____ to gain more information so I can transform this fear into a positive emotional state such as drive and determination."*

Such self-control also comes through the strengths of an effective support group of family and friends with whom you can share your thoughts. When you know someone really cares about you, negative emotions are more difficult to stimulate and sustain.

In summary: **Power thinking** channels negative emotions
(Levels 1–3 of the emotional scale) so their
energy is used to produce positive intentions,
actions, and thoughts.

The Positive Emotions

Level 4: Satisfaction from assuming responsibility. This emotional
level includes feelings of control, accomplishment, contentment,
and persistence. You will know that you are at this level when you
take action to overcome remorse and regret for wrongs done to
you or for your own unintentional actions that damaged yourself
or others. Level 4 also occurs when you engage in positive purposes.

Level 5: Drive and courage fueled by trust, faith and hope. This
emotional level is manifested in a desire and drive to create and
sustain positive purposes for others and yourself. One way to know
that you have reached this state is when you can believe in something so deeply that you are willing to sacrifice something of yourself for it.

Level 6: Joy and enthusiasm. This feeling begins when understanding or forgiveness occurs, or when appreciation is expressed.
Joy and enthusiasm stem from care and concern for others; these
evolve through a combination of *loss of self-centeredness* and *concern
for the well-being of others*. The most common reason for falling
from this emotional level is that you sabotage your own happiness
by exercising negative beliefs concerning love. However, when you
become a powerful thinker, you can manage the stresses as well as
the joys that loved ones and treasured goals bring into your life,
and your ability to sustain high spirits increases.

These three positive emotional levels can become permanent states,
sustaining insight and reason simultaneously. Repetition of positive emotions in close succession activates energy and fuses rationally perceived events with insight. They are like individual wires
which fuse into a single cable when encased in a protective, imper-

meable rubber cord. Moreover, when these cords multiply, they intensify the web of positive emotional states, insights, and reasonings; they become permanent aspects of your demeanor.

Another method of "keeping your spirits high" is to *seek truth*. If your view of the world is truthful, insight is not cluttered by illusions. Insight alone, without reason, cannot distinguish illusion from reality. When misperceptions unite with reasoning, the power of insight moves you to failure more rapidly than you would if you were not inspired. Therefore, the strategies for self-knowledge in Chapter 3 are very important when you are highly inspired to take immediate action.

CREATE AS MANY FLOW EXPERIENCES AS POSSIBLE

In his 1990 book *Flow*, psychologist Mihalyi Csikszentmihalyi at the University of Chicago describes optimal experiences as occurring:

> ... when we feel in control of our actions, [we feel ourselves to be] masters of our own fate and we feel a sense of exhilaration, a deep sense of enjoyment that is long cherished and that becomes a landmark in our memory for what life should be like.... Moments like these, the best moments in our lives, are not the passive, receptive, relaxing times... but usually occur when a person's body or mind is stretched to its limits in a voluntary effort to accomplish something difficult and worthwhile. It is something that we make happen! *Flow* is the state in which we are so involved in an activity that nothing else seems to matter; the experience itself is so enjoyable that people will do it at great cost, for the sheer sake of doing it.*

Total engagement, or *flow*, is a balance between the challenge and your ability to respond. If a challenge you face is beyond your

* Csikszentmihalyi, M. (1990). *Flow: The Psychology of Optimal Experience*, p. 3. New York: Harper & Row.

skills, your eventual frustration will result in worry and anxiety; if, on the other hand, your skills exceed the challenge of the task, boredom will ensue. Matching task challenges to your skills is essential to get maximum results from **power thinking**. When you do so, you create opportunities for incremental progress and receive information to measure your improvement instantly. Therefore, as you grow and learn through **power thinking,** you must continually take on new challenges in order to maintain your motivation. Such accomplishments provide satisfaction and feedback for further mastery. In this conception, the task "pulls" you, and ideally, you are working at the edge of your competence.

When athletes accomplish this in the course of a game, they experience "being in the zone." Everything they do is successful; opposition is stifled. This can occur for you, personally and professionally, when you become more aware of the conditions that place you at the edge of your competence. When you are there, your confidence and competence increase simultaneously.

☞ *To develop this awareness:* Recall a recent accomplishment that elicited your pride. This act must have involved the power thinking strategies you had learned to date, and a challenge you had not previously faced at so high a level. When you have this accomplishment in mind, recall what you did to reach your goal that was special. These actions should be present in your life on a more regular basis so that you can experience more flow states.

Flow also occurs when you arrange conditions that elicit your personally governed satisfaction, drive, courage and enthusiasm. Thus, after you complete monumental tasks, reflect on the positive emotions and insights that assisted your work. These should also be built into your life on a more regular basis if you are to enter more flow experiences.

Examples: Do you need to take frequent breaks and tell a few jokes prior to really engaging in a task? Do you need to be alone in a room? Do you need to know that minor difficulties have all been attended to? Do you need to have completed your exercise program? Whatever the conditions were that preceded your last flow experience, however insignificant they may appear, these are the conditions that need to be present as often as possible when you face large challenges.

With these supports in place, you have created a situation where flow can possibly begin. When it does, you will outperform those who are attempting the same challenge without the support of complete mental, emotional and physical unity toward an important goal. Procrastination and daily hassles obstruct flow because you distract your consciousness with reminder impulses that you have a commitment left unmet. Such postponing bars the complete mental immersion necessary for flow experiences.

In summary: The more often you *break away, maintain high spirits*, and arrange conditions so you move into *flow experiences*, the more powerful your insight becomes. The following questions can help you determine which stage of insight you need to improve. If you have experienced any of the following, we recommend that you review the pages we indicate. Doing so will enable you to select a specific method to strengthen your insight more rapidly.

1. *When reason turns to worry:* you need to *break away* before power thinking can proceed. Similarly, *when you cannot focus on a present goal or vision,* use *breaking away* to handle the major priorities in your life that are distracting you mentally.

 In the future, when you encounter either of these situations, what action(s) will you take to *break away*?

_____.

(For suggestions, reread pages 26–30.)

2. ***When you feel angry, afraid, or hurt:*** realize that these negative emotions need to be rechanneled by taking an action to *engage positive emotions* by assuming responsibility, so that you can unite insight and reason to overcome the challenge that life has presented.

 In the future, what action(s) will you take to *engage your positive emotions?*

_____.

(For suggestions, reread pages 30–36.)

3. ***When your level of attention to a task diminishes,*** or ***when fatigue sets in:*** arrange your situation so that you can move into a *flow experience.*

 In the future, what action(s) will you take to *create a flow experience?*

_____.

(For suggestions, reread pages 36–38.)

Looking ahead, be aware that when an activity engages your positive emotions, you also have an indication that you are working in an area of personal talent. Recognizing these talents through *self-knowledge* — the third dimension of powerful thinking — is the subject of our next chapter.

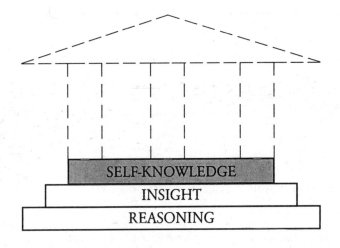

CHAPTER 3
A Foundation for Success: Self-Knowledge

Many people say that they want more out of life. To become a power thinker, reasoning to define correct paths of action and employing emotional inspiration and insight are not enough. You must work continuously to understand yourself and understand what drives your actions. Again, just as patience and conscious effort were essential in reasoning, and courage was necessary to activate insight, self-knowledge requires strong self-esteem. As Horace stated, "He who has confidence in himself will lead the rest" (*Epistle*, 65-80 BC). **Thinking Aid 5: Keys to Self-Knowledge** depicts seven strategies to increase your self-knowledge. Each of these strategies will be described in this chapter.

THINKING AID 5

KEYS TO SELF-KNOWLEDGE

KEEP YOUR SPIRITS HIGH

Keep Score

SELF-MOTIVATION, PASSION, DRIVE, AND HOPE

BELIEFS

TALENTS
MOTIVATION
NEEDS

SELF-CONCEPTS

PERSONAL ANALYSIS

DETERMINING YOUR PRESENT LEVEL OF SELF-ESTEEM

The following personal assessment will help you estimate your present level of self-esteem.

👉 To begin, write three words that accurately describe you at this point in time:

_____, _____, and _____.

👉 To complete the self-esteem assessment questionnaire, answer the following questions. After you have completed the questionnaire, we will describe the specific characteristic of self-concept that was analyzed in each question.

1. What do you say to yourself when you hear that you must do something with which you have little previous experience?

   _____

   _____.

2. Compared to your peers or co-workers, would you call yourself a risk-taker and/or a leader?

   ____ Yes, I judge myself to be a risk-taker and/or a leader.

   ____ No, I do not judge myself to lead or take as many risks as my peers.

   Why? _____.

3. When you are in a group and you share an idea that others agree is a good one, will you be the one to carry the idea to fruition, or will you wait until others ask to be involved and volunteer to do it?

   ____ I usually carry it to reality myself.

   ____ I postpone work on the idea until others are involved.

4. Do you think that others respect your abilities as much as you do?

   ____ yes   ____ no

   Why? _____

5. Which of the following types of comments do you receive most often?

____ Others tell me I could do more.

____ Others compliment me on things that I do that I value.

____ Others do not realize what my capabilities are.

____ Others compliment me on things that I do that I do not necessarily value that much.

6. Describe two situations in which you were timid in the past.

1. _____

_____

2. _____

_____

What was it specifically that decreased your courage?

_____

_____

7. List two situations, and the conditions that surrounded them, in which you took an action that required a lot of courage on your part.

_____

_____

_____

_____

_____

_____

What was it about these situations that made you overcome your timidity?

_____

_____

Do you want to transfer these qualities to more situations in which you could exercise courage, or were these situations not within your concept of yourself?

____ want to transfer

____ do not want to transfer

Explain your answer.

_____

_____

8. In the past, have you mastered most of the tasks and goals you established for yourself, or did you cease efforts before a goal was attained? Consider what you do when you realize that your talents are not up to a task.

    ____ I master most goals I set.

    ____ I give up on goals more frequently than I desire.

    ____ I finish tasks that are easy and within my talent range, but not those outside my areas of strength.

    What does the answer you checked above indicate, in your opinion?

    _____

9. Do you consider yourself a success?

    ____ yes   ____ no

    Why or why not?

    _____

    _____

    In what area(s) do you want to succeed to a larger degree?

    _____

10. Tell why success in the areas you listed in #9 is important to you at this time.

    _____

    _____

11. What effect does continuous criticism — or steady indifference — have upon you?

_____

What emotion(s) does it elicit?

_____

What question(s) does such an environment cause you to ask about yourself?

_____

_____.

12. Think of the last time you had self-doubt or felt insecure. What people were involved, and what were the circumstances?

_____

_____

_____.

What does this example demonstrate that can be used to strengthen a more positive sense of yourself?

_____

_____.

13. Thinking about these answers, what causes you self-doubt or insecurity?

_____

_____

✍ Now, reread your answers. How would you rate your self-concept?

____ as strong as I expected

____ neither strong nor weak

____ weaker than I desire

✍ What characterized situations that were most associated with a positive view of yourself? That is, in the questions to which you responded "yes," identify the patterns among the answers that led to positive feelings about yourself. For example, were you always self-determined in these situations? Did you use humor effectively? Was it cooperating well with others that led to the positive feelings you experienced about yourself?

_____

_____

_____

In the answers in which you related weaknesses, what was the common thread between/among these self-reports? For example, were you involved in similar situations when your confidence fell, or were you involved in activities that you do not value as highly as others?

_____

_____

Finally, describe the level of self-confidence you feel at this moment.

_____

_____

What do you think you can do to use your talents and motivations more frequently to raise your self-confidence and self-knowledge?

_____

_____.

The self-knowledge characteristics elicited by the above questionnaire are described in the Appendix at the end of this chapter. Check your answers to determine the strengths and weaknesses of your self-concept.

Now, reflect upon a situation in the recent past in which you were at your best, and when the best aspects of who you are were enacted. (Your self-esteem was high; you had increased ability to support good ideas; you organized new information rapidly; you performed exceptionally well for your own or others' welfare; you

promoted new ideas optimally; and/or, you led others effectively.)
The most important component of this experience was that you
created a situation in which *you knew how to receive what you truly
needed* to feel and become powerful, valued, and actualized.

In 1950, Abraham Maslow identified five basic human needs,
usually represented with a pyramid, as in **Figure 3-1** below. For
most of us, these needs fall within four categories.

- For some, what enables them to reach a high state of powerful thinking, productivity, and **self-actualization** (defined
  as feeling complete as a person) is *to feel truly loved*. If you
  are among these people, you will notice that your feelings
  of self-esteem rise in direct proportion to the degree to which

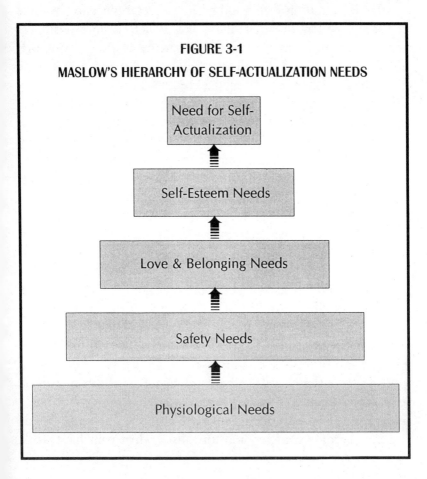

FIGURE 3-1

MASLOW'S HIERARCHY OF SELF-ACTUALIZATION NEEDS

Need for Self-Actualization

Self-Esteem Needs

Love & Belonging Needs

Safety Needs

Physiological Needs

you feel warmth, security, friendship, and caring.

- Alternatively, deeply-felt, sincere expressions of *appreciation of your work and self's worth* may be what enable you to reach higher levels of powerful thinking.
- Third, you may reach your highest levels of **power thinking** when you resolve or *understand a complex event*, establish the rationale for it, and realize that you played a major role in transforming a bewildering concept into a rational and usable form.
- Or you may become most powerful when you successfully *promote a new concept*, project, idea, person, or product that aided others, or *led a group to a positive result.*

While each of us feels good when we accomplish any of these goals, you will notice that one makes you feel more positively about yourself than the others and that the absence of one predictably lowers your high spirits and emotional energy. While these individualized needs will become clearer as you read further in this chapter, your insights about yourself can initially make your predominant emotional need known to you. For example, if you notice that you become less than your best when you begin to feel unwanted or unloved, your needs fall within the first category above. Alternatively, you may notice that most of your negative emotions emerge when you feel used and unappreciated (the second category). Or you may observe that you feel least powerful and most vulnerable whenever you do not understand something (the third category). Or, when you are unable to reach a new goal, promote ideas effectively, or lead others, you lose your motivation, drive, and self-esteem (the fourth category).

By sensitizing yourself to these feelings and their impact on how well or poorly you function, you can capitalize on your talents, beliefs, and motives to maximize your **power thinking** for yourself and others, as we will describe in Chapter 6. Becoming more aware of these needs lets you anticipate the effects of a given set of circumstances and take proactive steps to counter their negative impact. For example, if you have a need to be appreciated, you may become scattered and unrealistic when your hard work goes unnoticed. The strategies in this chapter enable you to understand the potential negative impacts of your feelings and to find new ways of rewarding your personal inclinations, preferences and strengths.

Strong self-knowledge is essential to **power thinking** and contains three components:

1. identifying your personal needs, talents, and motives;
2. analyzing your beliefs, and
3. strengthening your self-esteem.

When you know yourself well, you can "knock holes in the walls of new challenges" more rapidly than others, because you know which personal talents to exercise. The strategies we present will also enable you to identify talents you may not realize you have.

Before you read on, we encourage you to write the most important thing you want to improve in yourself. Specifying this self-improvement goal gives an immediate focus for you to consider and use the techniques that follow.

_____.

IDENTIFYING NEEDS, TALENTS, AND MOTIVES

Ways to help you identify your talents, needs and motives include:

☞ *Identifying the qualities of people in history that you admire.* When you identify the qualities of people in history whom you admire, and think about why you admire those qualities, you can discover core qualities in your personality that you may not have realized.

Before reading further, write the names of two or three people in history (or, if you prefer, of characters in movies or books) whom you admire.

_____

_____

Read through your list. What personality traits do these figures have in common?

_____

_____

_____

Write below any additional qualities you particularly admire in these people.

_____

_____

_____.

Do not read further until you have answered all three of these questions in writing.

Now, reread the sentences you wrote above. The traits you identified in these people are *qualities that you likely possess.* This is true because it is easier to see ourselves in others than it is to analyze ourselves as we are. Thus, the traits you admire in others are often those that you possess, whether you are aware of them or not. Therefore, when the actions of a historical, movie, or book character are personally memorable, it is because *you* have identified with that action and with the talents used. You generally identify with those who impress you in your daily life for the same reason. Therefore, by recognizing that you possess the character traits and talents you wrote about, you can use them more often in your daily activities. The resulting greater sense of who you are strengthens your confidence to handle more difficult challenges effectively. Doing so eliminates many obstacles before they arise. These are the reasons that powerful thinkers seem so sure who they are.

☞ *Finding a common element among people you enjoy being with* is a second method of understanding your personal qualities. Recognizing the qualities you enjoy in others may highlight dimensions of your personality for which you seek outside support, or personally strive to achieve. For example, if you enjoy being in groups when others do most of the talking, you could discover that oral expression is not your preferred means of communication. Writing may be more important to you. Similarly, if being in the presence of certain people creates security and peace, you may realize that achieving a sense of security is more important to you than claiming individual rewards and praise. You may also learn that having a sense of security is one of the conditions that must be present before you can attain more flow experiences.

✍ Whenever you feel out of touch with who you are, reflect upon the three people whose company you most enjoy. Write each person's name and the reasons why you enjoy being with him or her.

Name	*Reason*
1. _____	_____
2. _____	_____
3. _____	_____

Now, reread your list and try to identify the quality (or qualities) common to these people that bring you enjoyment.

_____

_____

_____

To review what you have done to strengthen your self-knowledge, know that what you have discovered to date are personal needs that must be addressed and talents that can be used to contribute more to yourself and others. By more frequently saying *yes* to situations in which you can satisfy these needs and exercise these talents, and *no* to situations in which you cannot, you will become a more powerful thinker. Also, by doing so, your subsequent activities will disclose even more self-knowledge and reveal other situations that bring out your best.

✍ Now, indicate how you can apply what you have learned about a personal quality you value to the self-improvement goal you wrote on page 49.

_____

_____

_____

☞ *Identifying the resources you most often call upon when you face challenges* is a third method to strengthen self-knowledge. By identifying resources (talents, thinking processes, or other people) that work well for you, you can utilize them more rapidly as supports when your initial plans falter or go awry.

✍ To identify your most valuable resources, think of a recent challenge you faced. List the supports you used to meet that challenge. Then rank them in order of the importance each holds for you (1 = most important, 2 = second most important, etc.).

(Rank)   *Support*

____ _____

____ _____

____ _____

____ _____

____ _____

____ _____

✍ What do the supports you ranked first and second tell you about yourself?

_____

What did this exercise suggest that you need in your life to become more productive?

_____

Do you have that now?   _____ yes _____ no

If not, where can you obtain this support more reliably in the future?

_____

In summary: Identifying and actualizing personal talents, motivations, and needs is the beginning of self-knowledge, the third foundation of **power thinking**. When inhibited from an immediate goal, you can return to the questions in this section of the book to identify a talent to employ in the next attempt. With these methods of continuously expanding self-knowledge in place, you can also strengthen self-knowledge by analyzing your beliefs.

EVALUATING YOUR BELIEFS

Beliefs are defined as the criteria, values or understandings you hold — which may or may not be based on facts — which influence the decisions you make and the actions you take. By evaluating your beliefs, you will understand an important dimension of your motivations. This will enable you to act less frequently on the basis of egocentricities, biases, or irrational desires. Unexamined beliefs impose limits upon self-knowledge because they are accepted uncritically as fact, so trying to analyze your beliefs may be difficult. Beliefs are nebulous — you often don't even realize why or how you came to view them as truths. In these cases, insight provides glimpses into the limits of a belief. The more you reason about a difficulty or problem you face, and visualize the actions you took, the more rapidly insight will reveal the motivation beneath the action. These motives frequently originate in your belief system. Once you can make conscious the beliefs you hold, and understand how they influence what you think and feel about a problem, you can use the strategies on the following pages to evaluate the positive and negative contributions your beliefs make to your life.

You should evaluate a belief when your conviction begins to seem unreasonable and/or does not feel right for who you are. Frequently such analysis reveals that rather than truly believing a specific belief, you have simply been *taught* to believe it.

Example: One plant manager firmly believed that "good managers do not hold too many meetings." Four months into his job, he felt a need to analyze this belief, and he did so using the strategies on the next pages. Essentially, he found that for *him* it was more effective not to hold too many meetings — but as a new leader of a group which didn't take initiative, his belief wasn't working. Instead of clinging to his counterproductive belief, the plant manager modified his conviction and began holding weekly meetings. The plant soon increased productivity above other divisions.

Example: You have been taught that an open-door policy at the office is best. However, you notice that people freely come in to chat at many times during the day. When you maintain the belief-based action, you do not complete your work and have to take it home. This leaves less time for your family. Analyzing the causes of your rising stress level can trigger the realization that your underlying belief in the open-door policy has negative consequences. You must re-evaluate your belief in light of this new self-awareness.

Example: You find yourself agreeing with your wife on most issues, even when you truly don't support some of her opinions, and you don't like the submissive feelings this causes. As you analyze your feeling, you realize that your actions are based on a belief that in the ideal marriage, husband and wife should discuss important issues until they can find a mutually pleasing solution. However, because your wife does not enjoy discussions and finds it difficult to compromise, you now find yourself conceding to her on too many issues. You don't like how you feel. This feeling and self-image enable you to identify the underlying belief that governed your actions. Understanding the belief allows you to make a rational choice between continuing or changing this behavior.

Rather than give additional examples, we ask that you pause now and identify a present situation interfering with your growth or with the attainment of some goal that you earnestly want to attain.

_____

_____

_____

Now write what beliefs or values motivate you to persist toward this goal.

_____

_____

_____

_____

_____.

Next, write the basis for these beliefs: Explain the likely cause for you coming to accept the belief as true for you (e.g., your parents held this belief and taught it to you, you read that this belief was important, etc.).

_____

_____

_____

How could you modify your belief so that it provides greater support to the reasoning and insights you have about why this goal is still elusive?

_____

_____

_____.

In the future, whenever you question the validity of a belief, you can also reference **Thinking Aid 6** (p. 57), and answer the following questions about the belief. Your answers will either more firmly establish that belief as a valuable component of your personality, or assist you to modify the belief so that it can contribute to your goals more effectively.

☞ *Step 1:* Does the belief you wrote above match your personality, needs and talents?

    ___ yes   ___ no

If so, this belief will stimulate one of the motivational drives in your personality; assisting you to:

- build closer relationships with people,
- establish trust,
- experience appreciation,
- reach new understandings, or
- produce new ideas/results.

How many incidents can you recall in which this belief assisted your growth in one of these ways? _____ Hampered it? _____

☞ *Step 2:* List ways this belief adds positively to your life.

_____

_____

If the belief is *not* making a positive contribution to your life, you will find that you cannot make such a list. Reasoning will not allow you to list positive experiences unless this belief indeed contributed to those experiences.

THINKING AID 6

EVALUATE YOUR BELIEFS

1. Does this belief match my past experiences, personality, talents, needs, and emotional makeup?

2. In what ways does this belief add positively to my life?

3. If someone challenges my beliefs, ask questions to make it easier for our beliefs to become compatible.

4. Choose beliefs that are most valid for me, instead of abandoning my beliefs in the face of others'.

☞ *Step 3:* Whenever your beliefs are challenged, *ask questions.* Do not offer a rational or emotional appeal in defense of your beliefs. For example, instead of arguing with someone about whether your beliefs are correct, ask others if they understand how your belief could be compatible with other beliefs they value in you; or ask what you can do to make your differing beliefs more compatible.

☞ *Step 4:* Choose beliefs that are most valid *for you:* those that bring you the most productivity, appreciation, results, and understanding. In Step 4, start to develop the ability to no longer be controlled by others who seek to change your beliefs, or by beliefs you acquired in the past which are no longer valid. When you value your own beliefs, you will no longer respond to pressures by altering the most treasured of them. Also, you will no longer accept someone else's word that a belief will carry truth for you as well as it does for them.

Example: One of the leading corporate presidents in the United States was advised to move his company's headquarters to another state. The move would save considerable taxes. Consultants pleaded and presented charts, statistics, and case histories in support of their advice. The president refused to move, however. This president "reasoned through his beliefs" and realized that he did not want to move because living in the house where his parents and grandparents had lived was very important to him. He believed that the factor of his personal happiness was more important to the success of his company than the increased profits that would accrue from a slightly lower tax rate. He chose not to move the headquarters. This president's belief proved superior to the more logical reasoning of those who gave unsolicited advice. His company became and remains one of the most profitable in its industry.

We are not implying that you should exclude the beliefs of others from *consideration*. However, your own beliefs should not be thrown aside merely for the purpose of reaching a compromise.

In summary: Evaluating your beliefs will allow you to (a) base actions on what *you* believe; (b) build your reasoning and insight with a sense of comfort, stability, and understanding, all of which builds your self-confidence; and (c) respond to your insights about yourself more knowledgeably and completely. You will know that you need to evaluate your beliefs when you do not understand why you are doing something, and when your confidence wanes. An invalid belief confuses your reasoning and pulls your insights in counter-productive directions. When your belief system is strong and in tune with your personal talents, needs, and motivations, your confidence increases, enabling you to reach your potential and to applaud others who do the same.

STRENGTHENING YOUR SELF-CONCEPT

The third strategy in developing self-knowledge is to nurture your sense of yourself — what psychologists refer to as your *self-concept*. A positive self-concept is developed through the successes of your early years of growing up, successful adult accomplishments, self-respect, a belief in your own worth, and confidence that you can overcome adversities. A healthy self-concept is manifested in a clarity of purpose that elicits the admiration of others. In addition, a strong self-concept initiates flow experiences and insight; creates more **STOP** reflections, **CAUTION**ed patience, and **CAP**ped speaking; and enables you to pursue more challenging commitments because your need for fear-induced self-protection is removed. You operate in these ways easily and naturally because you *know* these activities nurture your strong performances.

Our research supports the view that an optimistic sense of your ability to make positive changes also improves your psychological and physical well-being. Indeed, data indicate that the most successful innovators, the non-anxious, the non-despondent, and the social reformers take an optimistic view of their personal ability to make positive things happen, which enables them to exercise monumental influence over events that affect their own and others' lives. You can strengthen your self-concept in three ways:

- Completing the self-concept assessment questionnaire, which should help you understand yourself more clearly. (You have already completed this step in the beginning section of this chapter.)
- Removing the limitations you impose upon yourself.
- Keeping score!

Eliminating Self-Imposed Limitations

Another strategy for strengthening your self-concept is to eliminate limitations that you impose upon yourself. Why would any of us impose a negative quality or self-restricting limitation upon ourselves? We do it unintentionally because many of our self-imposed limitations are acquired at an early age. When we are young, we have a strong tendency to accept beliefs for irrational reasons: they are taught by our parents; we want to please someone we look up to; we are rewarded for believing certain things. Each time you accomplish a new and different thought or task (or a past task with greater success than you had expected), your capacity for a positive self-concept expands. Thus, in reality there is no such thing as a *limited capacity*. The concept you hold of yourself right now can increase in the next moment as the result of your current successful experiences. When you exceed a previous best, your sense of your own potential rises, and you see yourself as more capable than before. Such self-talk will engage your **power thinking**. More positive self-images, reasoning and intuition will also emerge.

In **power thinking**, regardless of the failures and successes of the past, the present is totally new. By using the strategies of **power**

thinking, you use your previous thoughts to increase the strength of the next thoughts and create totally positive possibilities for yourself. You recognize and control your own self-imposed limitations. Thus, every time you feel a negative thought about your capabilities, or reason that a limitation you imposed upon yourself is justified, you can turn to **Thinking Tool B** (below) and write answers to complete the statements. When you complete the last statement, it should have strengthened your resolve to overcome obstacles by engaging your personal talents, motivations, and positive beliefs. In addition, this writing activity directs your reasoning, insight, and emotions toward positive self-images and problem resolution.

Example: One Sunday evening Cathy and her husband returned from an out-of-town trip visiting her mother-in-law, who was ill. Cathy was tired, and she knows that fatigue reduces her **power thinking**. Sure enough, when she finished unpacking, she began to belittle herself

---

THINKING TOOL B

OVERCOMING SELF-IMPOSED LIMITATIONS

I feel _____ (state the emotion)

when I (you, it) _____
    (state what happened during the moment the emotion began)

I'm concerned that _____
    (tell what you don't want to occur in the future)

But I know it won't happen because I _____

_____

_____

---

with a barrage of negative self-talk: "If you weren't so lazy, you'd go into your office and begin working toward your deadlines right now!" "You've been gone all weekend and haven't accomplished a single thing toward your professional goals. You sure are falling behind, aren't you!" "Boy, if you don't work constantly you will never catch up!", etc., etc., and etc. When she heard these negative statements, she began to agree and impose self-limitations. As her sense of self depressed, she turned to **Thinking Tool B** and wrote:

I feel tired, emotionally drained, and confused
When I chose not to compose on the computer tonight.
I'm concerned that I will fall behind in my work;
But I know it won't happen because I control my deadlines; I will not produce something that isn't my best; and, I will have increased energy tomorrow morning to regain time toward the deadlines I have set for myself.

Through this strategy, Cathy increased her positive sense of herself, removed her negative thinking, and gained peace and strength from the subsequent two hours that she spent unwinding. During that *break-away* time, she also mentally restructured the next day's priorities, and had an insight that improved the book she was writing.

Self-imposed limitations can also arise when you do not daily assess the value of your personal worth. Specifically, when you place the needs of others far above your own, you limit your capacity to expand your own talents, beliefs, and motivations. Such limitations suppress the power that self-knowledge can deliver in **power thinking**. In addition, denying yourself for a long period of time can create a self-imposed longing that could eventually surface and interfere with a future goal.

You may be sabotaging your self-concept in tiny ways as well. You may create hassles and problems because you do not value your needs, talents, beliefs, and motivations highly enough.

Example: Our friend Frank used to receive frequent parking and
            speeding tickets — until he realized that he valued
            the image of himself as a good driver, and that the
            hassles created by the tickets were too distracting to
            his goals. Therefore, to avoid incurring those hassles
            and creating a situation that decreased his self-image,
            he *changed his driving and parking patterns*. He has
            not received any tickets for parking or driving viola-
            tions for several years.

✍ As a final thought about self-imposed limitations, write something you want to change about yourself.

   _____

   _____

   _____

✍ Now complete the statements presented in **Thinking Tool B**
   relative to that self-image. After you have finished, return to
   read the rest of this page.

   I feel _____ *(state*
   the emotion)

   when I (you, it) _____
   (state what happened during the moment the emotion began)

   I'm concerned that _____
   (tell what you don't want to occur in the future)

   But I know it won't happen because I _____

   _____.

   Sometimes analyzing a limitation with **Thinking Tool B** will
not elicit the actions you can take to overcome it. In such instances, the reason this limitation exists is that it has an underlying good intention that you value. For instance, *gullibility,* often
viewed as a limitation or negative trait, is rooted in a strong positive belief in the *value* of extending trust to others. Therefore,
before you can eliminate some self-imposed limitations, you must

place healthy boundaries on positive talents, needs, values, beliefs, or motivations (e.g., "To avoid being taken advantage of, what can I do by engaging **CAUTION**ed reasoning in situations where my trust can be extended?"). Unless you identify the value that you are carrying to an extreme, you can fool yourself into believing that you wish to change qualities which, in truth, you value.

Example: In a research study, people were given a list of nega-
           tive qualities, such as "selfishness," being a "penny-
           pincher," etc. They were asked to indicate whether
           each item was a characteristic they possessed, and/or
           one they had tried to change but could not. Then, the
           psychologists phrased each item in a more positive
           manner, and asked subjects if they valued that quality
           in themselves, such as asking if "thrift" was important
           to them. Results suggested that those negative charac-
           teristics that people wanted to change, but apparently
           could not, were actually *traits that they valued in them-
           selves* when these characteristics were called by a more
           positive name.

Therefore, many self-imposed "limitations" can be removed by understanding the positive qualities that underlie that value, and using **STOP** and **CAUTION** to employ it in positive ways.

Similarly, when you are feeling sorry for yourself, you can alter these self-images by *doing the reverse of what you sense you want.* For example, when you want someone to give you something, instead give something to yourself or someone else. "Doing the opposite" does not necessarily mean that you give the same thing you wanted to receive, nor do you have to give to the person from whom you wanted to receive something, in order for feelings of self-pity to cease.

Example: Phyllis loves to receive flowers. Her husband does
           not value buying her flowers. Therefore, Phyllis ap-
           plied this strategy to her life and began giving more to
           friends at the office. They reciprocate with trinkets and
           flowers. Thus, instead of allowing a difference in be-

liefs between herself and her husband to lower her self-concept, or bemoaning the fact that her husband was "not the romantic type," she changed her thoughts of self-pity by doing the reverse of what she felt her self-concept deserved. In essence, she gave to herself by giving to others. Her self-image expanded because giving was one of her strongest motivators and talents. Others benefited — and as an unintended outcome, she now receives flowers often.

Keeping Score

The third strategy to strengthen your self-concept is to use a scoreboard. You could be winning and not know it if you aren't keeping score! One of the most important long-term supports for a self-concept is to "keep score" and challenge yourself to improve. By setting goals, you become so involved in personal development that you have limited time to engage in negative self-talk.

The Power of Positive Students (POPS) Center in Denver, Colorado, reported that only three people in every hundred write their goals — and that the people who write their goals achieve at least fifty percent more than those who do not. By writing goals, you can truly focus because nebulous dreams become written realities. Moreover, the writing process places the goal into your subconscious, closer to your insight. In doing so, you remain alert to new opportunities others offer. Such mental focusing does not occur as readily when you merely say your goals to yourself (or others), or when your goals remain global desires and daydreams.

To begin keeping score, *write your goals* using the steps depicted in **Thinking Tool C** on the next page. You should write your goals in a predictable location, such as on a notepad or calendar that you use daily. Force yourself to review your goals or objectives each day. To get yourself into this habit:

✍ First, *write* a goal you want to achieve by the end of this week.

✍ Second, *develop* a plan of action to reach that goal. This plan states the reasoned methods you will use to attain your goal.

Such a plan keeps you from ignoring inconvenient and annoying details, or omitting small but important responsibilities. You develop an action plan for the goal you wrote by writing what you will accomplish each day and how long it will take. (Remember that your goal is just for this week.)

☞ Third, *visualize* how you will feel when your goal has been reached. Taking the time to picture how you will feel when your goal is reached will help to initiate insight, engage your talents to work on the goal, and make your goal more specific. When goals are as specific as possible, it is easier to believe they can be achieved.

☞ Last, *state* a day or time when your goal will be reached. This deadline makes the plan more challenging and fun to achieve.

Example: Cathy often refers to her husband as her coach. He taught her how to jog and watches when she lifts weights to ensure correct form. They enjoy their Saturday afternoons together when he "coaches" her. However, it would have been tempting to let other priorities and interruptions interfere with this somewhat demanding routine, so they "keep score." They established a goal and set a date on which they would measure the results of their weekly workouts.

Finally, when your deadline arrives, analyze why the goal was or was not attained. With this reflective step, you will automatically learn more from your failures, increase the probability of future success, and set higher quality goals in the future.

As a summary of the "keeping score" strategy, we quote a poem originally composed by Roger Mager:

> To rise from a zero
> To a big campus hero
> The answers to three questions
> You must surmise:
> *Where are you going?,*

THINKING TOOL C
SETTING POWERFUL GOALS

Step 1: Write It Down!
Goal: _____

Step 2: Plan of Action

1. _____
   _____

2. _____
   _____

3. _____
   _____

4. _____
   _____

Step 3: How Will I Know I Have Reached My Goal?

Step 4: Set A Deadline! _____

How will you get there?, and
How will you know that you have arrived?

CONCLUSION

You now have the foundation for powerful thinking in place. You can reason to make ideas practical. You can use *insight, breaking away, high spirits*, and *flow experiences* to inspire new ideas. You can complete personal assessments for greater *self-knowledge* to achieve higher ideals more effectively and efficiently. In Chapters 4–6, we will apply **power thinking** to situations in which you must make decisions, solve problems, and change.

However, before you read on, we ask that you respond to the questions and activity below.

✍ What do you think the self-esteem assessment at the beginning of this chapter revealed about you?

_____

_____

✍ What new self-knowledge for growth do you now want to achieve?

_____

_____

✍ Pause for a moment and use **Thinking Tool C** to begin "keeping score" toward this growth. Write your goal and plan of action. This is your first step to engage the continuous self-knowledge growth component in your **power thinking**.

APPENDIX
Explaining the Self-Esteem Questions

Questions 1 and 2 were designed to assess your *self-efficacy*: the strength of your belief that you can overcome adversities. Leaders in human resource development and researchers exploring self-concept have concluded that people with the strongest self-knowledge more frequently take risks and seek to improve themselves, others and situations by leading improvements (within their range of talents) without being asked to do so. These people's answers to question 1 would be positive and confident to learn and discover. If you answered question 1 with any sense of trepidation, you can increase your self-efficacy by identifying and developing more of your talents.

Question 3 was designed to assess your internal locus of control, which means the degree to which you believe you cause positive events in your life. If you answered that you "usually carry ideas to reality," you believe your personal power and effort are valuable. If you answered that you "postpone implementation until others are involved," you have a less firm sense of personal control. It could be that you attribute too much of your personal success to luck, circumstances or the input of others.

Question 4 was designed to assess how well you demonstrate and communicate your talents and self-knowledge to others. If you answered "yes," you will waste fewer moments and use less energy explaining your actions and thoughts to others than will your peers who feel others don't give them the respect they deserve or misunderstand them. If you wish to increase the amount of respect you command, the first step is to demonstrate to others the qualities that you respect in yourself. For example, if you respect your generous nature, give to others more.

In doing so, be aware that some may try to persuade you that this essential strength is actually a weakness — e.g., for generosity, "You are a pushover," "Others will take advantage of you if you don't look out for number one first," etc. Being true to the aspects of yourself that you admire, regardless of some people's negative interpretations, allows you to attract more people who value these same qualities. When this occurs, the synergy that will develop in the work you do together will bring you to high levels of success, and you will become more personally fulfilled.

Question 5 was designed to assess if you are working within your areas of talent. If you chose option 2, you are projecting the talents that you value. Most people should understand your personality.

Questions 6 and 7 were designed to identify situations that do not use your own talents, and may even call upon you to enact beliefs that you consider wrong. By rereading your answer to question 6, you can reflect upon the validity or invalidity of the underlying value and/or belief that requires your courage to enact. Because life may place you in such situations more frequently than you desire, you can call upon the motive you wrote in question 7 to muster the courage to progress positively in such situations.

Question 8 was designed to determine if you have a lot of incomplete cycles of effort in your life. If you answered that you "cease effort more frequently than you desire," it could indicate that your insight and emotions are being drained because you place energy into many uncompleted thoughts, actions and desires. Such dissipation increases the likelihood that future actions will not result in positive closure. Your self-knowledge can assist by identifying simple tasks that are on your mind from the recent past that you can complete today. When you complete one, you will experience a resurgence of energy for other challenges.

Questions 9 and 10 were designed to analyze your self-image. If you answered "yes" to question 9 and wrote several areas of desired improvement, your self-image is contributing positively to **power thinking**. Question 10 was designed to help you gauge the amount of focus in your life, and to possibly reveal situations that reduce your self-image.

Question 11 was designed to help you identify your motives and personality type. The answers to the questions in item 11 also identified the most powerful contributor to your lowered self-concept.

Questions 12 and 13 were designed to identify an inner resource you can call upon whenever self-doubt emerges.

Refer to **Thinking Aid 7** (on the facing page) to remind you to draw on the different elements of your self-knowledge.

THINKING AID 7
UNITING REASON AND INSIGHT TO KNOW MYSELF BETTER

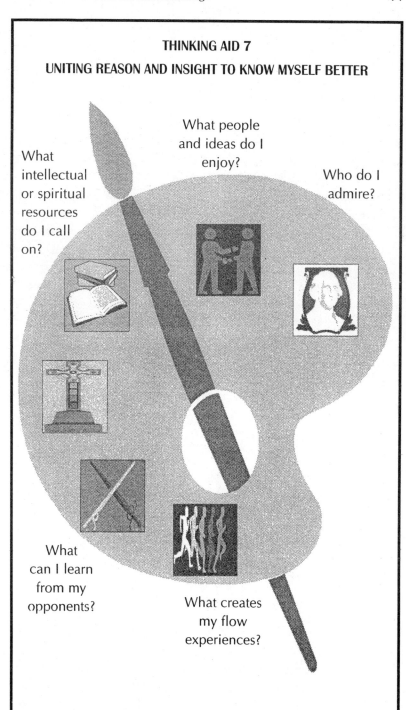

What people and ideas do I enjoy?

What intellectual or spiritual resources do I call on?

Who do I admire?

What can I learn from my opponents?

What creates my flow experiences?

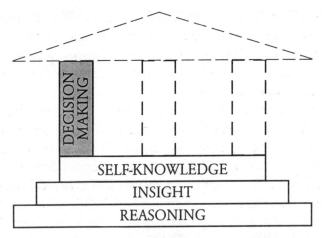

Reasoning:
STOP: read/reflect/write
DOUBLE THINK
CAUTION: listen/ask questions
*WEIGHTED
CHARACTERISTICS TEST*
GO: CAPped Speech
*REPLACE EXCUSES WITH
EXPLANATIONS*

Insight:
Break Away
COMMIT
High Spirits
*AWAIT GOOD
INDICATORS*
Create Flow
THROUGH PR

Self-Knowledge:
Talents/Needs/Motives
CONQUER HUMAN NATURE
Analyze Beliefs
*ANALYZE BELIEFS ABOUT
SAYING YES AND NO*
Strong Self-Concept
*MONITOR YOUR SELF-
RESPECT*

CHAPTER 4
Power Thinking and Decision Making

A *good decision* permits the most positive progress within the context of variables known at the time of decision. You may be as
surprised as we were to discover that *only 12%* of decisions made

in business today meet this standard. We contend that success requires **power thinking** and use of the special tools we have listed in the graphic above. Such **power thinking** restrains negative vacillation and expands constructive contemplation — both necessities in making good decisions.

The purpose of this chapter is to describe nine **power thinking** tools. First, we present the tools that build reasoning power during decision making. Powerful reasoning for decision making means that you not only **STOP** to read, reflect, and write, but DOUBLE THINK. You process thoughts with **CAUTION** by listening, asking questions, *and* completing a WEIGHTED CHARACTERISTICS TEST. You speak *C*oncisely, *A*ccurately, and *P*recisely (**CAP**), and REPLACE EXCUSES WITH EXPLANATIONS. In the second and third sections of the chapter, we describe three tools that strengthen insight, and three that build your self-knowledge during decision making. Used together, these strategies will increase the number of good decisions you make every day.

REASONING DURING DECISION MAKING

Stage I: Double Thinking

When you **STOP** to read, reflect, and write during decision making, we encourage you to refer to and answer the questions on the DOUBLE THINK CHECKLIST (**Thinking Tool D**, pp. 76–78). **Thinking Aid 8**, on the next page, will help remind you to do a DOUBLE THINK. DOUBLE THINKING lets you:

- imagine positive outcomes,
- select preferred alternatives,
- adopt a long-term perspective, and
- experiment with options before taking action.

Without DOUBLE THINKING, choosing among options can cause too much stress. You may miss the most optimal resolution because no matter what you do, the fear that other choices might have been better looms over you. These nagging fears distract your reasoning. The checklist also limits the use of unproductive short-

THINKING AID 8: DO A DOUBLE THINK BEFORE DECIDING

- Imagine
  I am on
  their side

- Look at
  my own
  side

cuts and overreliance on past experiences during decision-making. While insight and past experiences should be one piece of information, prior knowledge may contain irrelevant or outdated assumptions, may not reflect the current reality, is devoid of your recent growth as a person, and does not account for new information or factors unique to the situation at hand.

As you are aware, some decisions are made within a few seconds. Others are pondered. When you must carefully consider your decision, referencing the questions on the DOUBLE THINK CHECKLIST as early as possible in your decision-making process will move you to an active process of identifying the critical elements involved in this decision and working on narrowing the choices to the critical one(s) — the one(s) on which you ultimately decide.

✍ To understand the power of this thinking tool, even on your first reading, write on the following lines a decision you face right now:

_____

Now, as you read the Checklist for the first time, answer each question as it relates to this decision. For each question that you answer *no*, consider using the strategies for **power thinking** we discussed in Chapters 1-3.

✍ Write the two or three preferred options that emerged from this process.

_____

_____

_____

✍ Did you have any insight about your decision?

_____

_____

_____

THINKING TOOL D
THE ELEMENTS OF EFFECTIVE DECISION-MAKING:
THE DOUBLE THINK CHECKLIST

1. Do I have enough information now to make this decision?

   ___ yes   ___ no

   If not, how can I get the information required to make this decision?

2. Do I know what I need or want from this decision?

   ___ yes   ___ no

   If not, I must wait until I do. If so, how can I use my motivation and talents to receive it without causing damage to other positive purposes?

   _____

3. Can I test alternative choices on a small scale, or seek advice from an expert in the field before I decide?

   ___ yes   ___ no

4. What could I do to make this decision easier and more effective? For example, what have I used in the past to make similar decisions? Write a letter to the people involved to "write away my negative thoughts" and then not mail it? Talk to significant others to gain new perspectives? Take longer to decide? Establish a time in the future when I will reassess conditions around the decision, until I have good indicators that the optimal time for making the decision has arrived?

   _____

5. Have I imagined what will occur if each possible alternative is implemented?

   ___ yes   ___ no

THINKING TOOL D (CONTINUED)

6. Have I considered all the people who will be affected and the viewpoints of both women and men?

   ____ yes   ____ no

7. Have I developed a back-up plan in case the result I expect does not come about?

   ____ yes   ____ no

7a. Is there a risk involved?

   ____ yes   ____ no

   If so, what support do I have? _____

   If there is a risk involved, are my chances greater than 50/50 that positive outcomes will result if I decide now?

   ____ yes   ____ no

8. Am I basing my decision solely on past experiences?

   ____ yes   ____ no

9. Is this the right time to make the decision?

   ____ yes   ____ no

   Can I take more time to think, e.g.: "Could I call you tomorrow after I've had time to think about it? What time would be the best to reach you?"

   ____ yes   ____ no

10. Have I fully assessed alternatives that I might have discarded too quickly?

   ____ yes   ____ no

11. Have I considered how Murphy's Law ("Anything that can go wrong will go wrong") could impact the outcome of each of the choices I am considering?

   ____ yes   ____ no

THINKING TOOL D (CONTINUED)

Considering the Law of Averages, what are the best and the worst possible outcomes of each option?

_____

12. If I take the first option (and it turns out to be the best decision), what is the greatest good that could be accomplished? _____

_____

If I take the second option, what is the greatest good that could be accomplished? _____

_____

13. Do I feel that it is less threatening to suspect than it is to know for sure? Therefore, am I putting off making a decision to keep from "knowing for sure"?

____ yes   ____ no

14. Is this *my* decision and my responsibility, or am I trying to make someone else's decision?

____ yes   ____ no

15. Have my feelings on this matter affected my choice of an option?

____ yes   ____ no

If yes, in a positive or negative direction? _____

Alternatively, have my emotions of anger, doubt, or fear minimized my opportunity that exists in taking an action? _____ yes _____ no

16. Can I think of only one course of action? _____ yes _____ no

If so, I will proceed through these questions again until other possible alternatives emerge, to make sure I am not overlooking options.

As you read, you likely identified some questions you felt were especially useful in this process. With practice, you should learn to ask these particular questions automatically, before you make decisions too quickly. Doing so enables you to isolate alternatives, forcing you to consider different courses of action before you decide on one. The ultimate decision will be more considered and thus probably better.

Example: To illustrate how integral DOUBLE THINKING can become, we want to tell you about a corporate leader, who is our friend and an excellent DOUBLE-THINKER. When the DOUBLE THINK CHECKLIST reveals that more information is needed, actions are delayed until he can access this knowledge. When he thinks through a decision, he thinks out loud or with actions.

For instance, during implementation of group decisions, he stops by subordinates' offices, asking the DOUBLE THINK questions to find what else is needed before a deadline arrives. Through his modeling, the DOUBLE THINK process of "immediate thinking" and "delayed thinking" is taught to his subordinates by example.

In the future, when you ponder a decision, we encourage you to refer to this checklist as you consider all the elements of the problem(s) you must resolve. The answers you develop will give you insight into the nature of the issues involved in the problem, and identify some options or alternatives. Once you have identified them, you can assess their merits. This stage of the decision-making process involves generating information and options, and also considering how your emotions may be influencing the process. Your search is for as much information as you can gain, and time in which to read, reflect about the options you have identified, and listen attentively to the various viewpoints about these options. You should also complete a weighted characteristics test.

Stage II: Complete a Weighted Characteristics Test

A *weighted characteristics test* is a method of thinking about the interaction of many causes and variables within a challenging situation, so you can see the total picture of the outcomes that could occur with each option you are considering. **Thinking Aid 9** (on the facing page) will remind you to use this **power thinking** strategy. To begin the test:

✍ Write a phrase that describes one of your preferred options on the left side of the balance scale and a phrase for an alternative preferred option on the right side.

✍ Then, on the lines inside these scales, list the positive outcomes that could occur if each decision was made, based on your current knowledge of the variables. To keep the scale accurate, write the negative outcomes of each option by phrasing them as *positive* outcomes of the *other* option — because choosing the opposite will give you the benefit of avoiding that negative outcome.

✍ After writing all the possible consequences, count the total number of the statements you wrote on both sides. Then, select the outcome or consequence most important to you, and write the number of the total in the blank to the right of that consequence. For example, if you wrote 10 possible outcomes, the number to the right of your most important outcome would be 10.

Next, find the consequence that is second in importance to you and assign it the next lower number. (In our example, you would write 9 in the blank to the right of that consequence.) Continue in this manner until all consequences on both sides of the scale are assigned a number in order of their importance for *you*. Last, total the number of points of all statements on both sides of the balance. The option with the highest score is the best decision you can make at this time.

One of the benefits of this approach is that it enables you to see what your values really are. To demonstrate, we ask you to

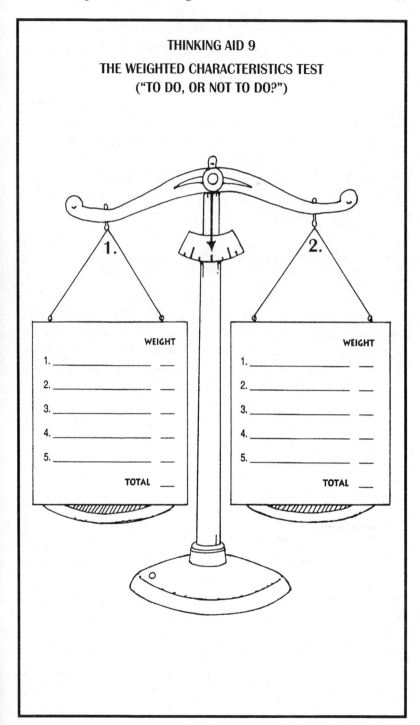

THINKING AID 9

THE WEIGHTED CHARACTERISTICS TEST
("TO DO, OR NOT TO DO?")

pretend you are faced with the following decision. Use this weighted characteristics method with **Thinking Tool E** (on the facing page) to see how you would decide on an option, and let's see how our weighting differs from yours. Here's the situation:

☞ You have been offered a new job. You and your family have deep roots in the town in which you presently live and the job will require a move across the United States. It will double your salary. You will receive a substantial annuity. The company is internationally known. This is the job you've wanted all your life. Your wife is reluctant to move. Your son is a sophomore in high school. The climate is not as good in the new location, and commuting time to work is considerably longer.

After you have identified your possible options (*move* or *do not move*), identified the characteristics of each situation, decided on the importance to you of each statement, and totaled the scores of both options, look at our solution in **Figure 4-1** on page 84 to see how your rankings compare with ours.

✍ Now, to practice this method a second time, rethink the decision that you wrote on page 75, using the weighted characteristics method to analyze your options.

Once you understand how to use the weighted characteristics method during the **CAUTION** step of reasoning, you may modify it. Some power thinkers visualize the scale in their minds and weigh outcomes without writing; others list pros and cons only without assigning a numerical weight to each factor. The essence of this method is to pit alternatives against one another so the best choice can be tempered into strong resolution.

Armed with the results of this weighted characteristics test, you have identified several reasons you made the decision you did. When you state these reasons along with your decision, you can indicate what factors influenced your options and ultimate

THINKING TOOL E
THE WEIGHTED CHARACTERISTICS TEST

DO _____ :   DO **NOT** _____ :

1. _____   1. _____
   _____   _____
   _____ __   _____ __
2. _____   2. _____
   _____   _____
   _____ __   _____ __
3. _____   3. _____
   _____   _____
   _____ __   _____ __
4. _____   4. _____
   _____   _____
   _____ __   _____ __
5. _____   5. _____
   _____   _____
   _____ __   _____ __
6. _____   6. _____
   _____   _____
   _____ __   _____ __
7. _____   7. _____
   _____   _____
   _____ __   _____ __
8. _____   8. _____
   _____   _____
   _____ __   _____ __

TOTAL _____ __   TOTAL _____ __

FIGURE 4-1

This is how we completed the test and weighted the advantages and disadvantages. How did our responses compare to yours?

MOVE		DO NOT MOVE	
1. Double my salary	10	1. Value of deep roots	4
2. Substantial annuity	5	2. Wife will be happier	9
3. Internationally known firm	6	3. Son could finish school	8
4. Always wanted this job	7	4. Climate is better here	1
5. Commute could give me time to work on subway	3	5. Commute could take time from family	2
TOTAL	**31**	**TOTAL**	**24**

---

choice; your **CAP**ped speech enables decisions to be communicated more easily. This brings us to the third stage and our next thinking aid in decision making: telling others about your decisions effectively by *replacing excuses with explanations*.

Stage III: Replace Excuses with Explanations

Excuses come in two forms: those we give others and those we give ourselves. Both can have destructive outcomes. In this section, you will learn to replace excuses with explanations and to communicate explanations to others powerfully before stating your decisions.

Webster's New World Dictionary defines an **excuse** as "*a pretended reason for conduct intended to excuse oneself from responsibility.*" **Explanations** are *statements of reasons that support one's conduct.* The difference between these two concepts is significant. When you feel a need to excuse yourself from a past action, we encourage you to offer an apology instead. At present, you may give excuses rather than apologies because, on the surface, excuses appear easier. Making true statements of the reasons why we behave as we do requires *courage* — courage to accept the fact that we are not perfect, and courage to risk having our true, deeply held reasons for action rejected. It takes bravery to state, "Because of _____ , I decided not to do _____ ," rather than "I really, really wanted to do it but (someone won't let me) or (X occurred — which may be true or invented)."

Moreover, although you may think excuses help to temporarily avoid something harmful, they do not. Giving excuses has a negative outcome: it increases the frequency with which others make requests of you that you do not want to accept! When you give an excuse, people believe that your excuse is the real reason you are declining their request. Therefore, in the future they will make the same request again because they believe that you really wanted to do it, and if they just plead more urgently, you will overcome your past obstacle (such as being "too tired," or "so busy"). After all, everyone gets rested and slows down sometime! All they have to do is to continually re-ask until they discover when this opportune time is for you.

Alternatively, an excuse-free, *C*oncise, *A*ccurate, and *P*recise (**CAP**ped) reason for having made a decision will protect you from the "rain and hail" of *untrustworthiness* that excuses generate. Excuses create a mismatch between your non-verbal language and your words. For instance, while you say how sorry you are for not meeting someone's request, your non-verbal language demonstrates that you could have met the request if desired. Therefore, when you make excuses, power thinkers will notice the discrepancy and judge you to be inconsistent — or even dishonest. By stating the *explanation* for your decision, you make yourself more trustworthy. In the future, others will more highly prize your agreement to meet their request, since they know you truly want to do so. You are not meeting it merely out of a social obligation or because you lacked an effective excuse not to do so.

Also, by stating reasons for your decisions, you will not waste mental and physical energy trying to create — and remember —

believable excuses. Excuse-giving can become a strategy for avoiding reality, which will distract your subconscious and decrease the power of insight. Because subconscious mental processes cannot discern excuses from true statements, excuses make your subconscious attend to both excuses and reality simultaneously as fact. Insight, like a laser beam, can travel best in the straight path that unobstructed truth provides.

Equally destructive are the excuses you give yourself. As you see from the list in **Thinking Tool F** (on the facing page), excuses you give yourself are usually negative self-affirmations, e.g., "I can't because I'm so fat," "I don't have time," "I forgot," "I couldn't do that because...." When you use them, you demean yourself. If you use an excuse too frequently, you convince yourself that you really cannot accomplish a goal because of the excuse you created.

To reiterate: *Excuses block your ability to assume larger responsibilities and face challenges honestly.* And, as we discussed in Chapter 3, honesty is an important ingredient in strengthening insight. If you have put in the effort to read this far, we trust you will want to eliminate the harmful impact of excuses on your **power thinking** and decision making. You can eliminate excuses in three steps.

- First, use the DOUBLE THINK checklist to reduce your vacillation and vulnerability, because you know and identify the elements that are relevant for a decision choice.
- Second, complete **Thinking Tool E** (the Weighted Characteristics Test) to weight these elements, identifying the true reasons why *you* committed to your decisions.
- Third, identify the excuses you are most tempted to give and why. Use **Thinking Tool F** to understand what it is about certain situations that makes you afraid to present your true self through reality-based explanations.

We suggest that you display **Thinking Aid 10** (page 88) in a prominent, but private place and that you review the list in **Thinking Tool F** several times each week. Read the list now to identify the most common excuses you have used in the past. Once you have identified the excuse you use most frequently, write a statement

THINKING TOOL F

WRITING STATEMENTS THAT REPLACE EXCUSES

I CAN'T/DON'T BECAUSE... I CAN AND WILL BECAUSE...

1. I've done it before and it didn't work, or it (or I) wasn't good. _____

2. No one told me that it was OK to begin. _____

3. That isn't my job. _____

4. I'm too busy or tired. _____

5. I don't have time. _____

6. I forgot to. _____

7. I didn't know it was so important. _____

8. It was already good enough for them so it should be good enough for me. _____

9. I just can't seem to get started. _____

10. I would if I just didn't have so much to do right now. _____

11. _____ isn't worth the time, energy or effort. _____

12. It bores me. _____

13. I'll do it later. _____

14. I'm too fat/ugly/lazy/etc. _____

15. I have too many responsibilities at _____. _____

16. If I were in complete control of my time, I'd _____. _____

17. It makes me feel uncomfortable. _____

18. I don't want to. _____

THINKING TOOL F (CONTINUED)

19. It wasn't important.   _____

20. I'm scared, ashamed or mad.   _____

21. I can't find _____.   _____

22. _____   _____

23. _____   _____

THINKING AID 10
WINNERS DO NOT GIVE OR USE EXCUSES!

you can use in the future as an effective substitute for that excuse on the line to the right of the excuse. To do so, recall past situations in which you offered that excuse. Could you have made these situations (1) more comfortable, (2) less fearful, (3) more slowly paced, or (4) more secure, so that you wouldn't have needed an excuse to avoid doing something?

☞ For excuses you give yourself, you can begin this statement with the words:

"*I can* _____ [a positive action you will take to counteract your negative self-affirmation] *whenever I* _____ [describe the situations in which you are tempted to use that specific negative self-affirmation]."

The following are examples we and others have used and recommend:

1. "It sounds like a wonderful opportunity [great fun, valuable experience] and I bet [another person's name] would like to go in my place. I am not going to agree to do it because _____."
2. "You are such a good social director for us that I never worry that our next activity will be just as much fun [as valuable] as this one. I am glad that you always ask me to be included because some people may not ask again if I had declined in the past. I am not coming this time because _____."
3. "You are such a special friend because you know that my saying *no* does not mean I don't consider the activity to be valuable or that I don't value you. I look forward to your next call."
4. "Could I do the task at a different time?"
5. "Would it be helpful if I suggested someone to take my place?"
6. "I don't enjoy _____ , but thank you."
7. "It's not my top priority and I want to focus on my top priority."

To close this description of strengthening your **CAP**ped speech, we encourage you to read **Thinking Tool F** frequently. It can help you remove more subtle excuses, and with each revisit, you will increase your strength to speak truthfully.

In summary: Reflecting, reading, writing, DOUBLE THINKING, and the Weighted Characteristics Method can aid you in:

- actively analyzing the elements that go into solving a problem;
- identifying the possible options; and
- weighting their relative values for you.

These can help you identify the most desirable decisions. Then, using **CAP**ped speech without excuses makes your reasoning more trustworthy. With these **Thinking Aids** in action, once a decision is made, you and others will also remain more loyal to that decision. You and they will judge it positively, even if it does not prove to be as successful as you had hoped. This is an important component in making good decisions, and brings us to the next **power thinking** tool — *making strong, valid commitments.* Doing so engages your insight and inspiration.

INSIGHT DURING DECISION MAKING

Stage I: Making Positive Commitments

As you are already aware, making and keeping commitments is easier for some people than others. The purpose of this section is to give you cause either to congratulate yourself for overcoming obstacles that limit others' own personal commitment abilities, or to take action to increase your commitment ability.

Have you already noticed that when you commit to a project, the work becomes easier? The reason for this effect is that commitment *focuses* your rational energy and inspires insight to persevere toward a clearly identified target. Once you commit, your subconscious no longer has to consider different directions simultaneously, e.g.: "If I do A, then B will happen; if I do X, then Y will happen." Furthermore, if you have developed the habits of (a) keeping appointments, (b) fulfilling promises, and (c) maintaining confidences, we feel certain that these actions will have established a self-image inconsistent with indecisive behavior.

As you strengthen your ability to commit, remember that making positive commitments takes courage. Such fortitude arises from deeply held convictions which take time to develop and verbalize. **Thinking Aid 11** (on the next page) has been designed to remind you of this strategy.

We have found that it takes time for insight and self-knowledge to attach to rationally selected targets. If you already "break away" to analyze your feelings so that insight and inspiration can intervene in decision making, we commend you.

On the other hand, if "breaking away" to form positive commitments is difficult for you, we provide **Thinking Tool G** (pp. 93-94) to help signal your need to break away, rest, and revitalize so positive commitments can be made. As you reflect and write answers to the following questions, we suggest that you write today's date in the blank that precedes each statement. By doing so, you can "keep score" about growth in overcoming causes of non-commitment. In the blank that follows each statement, write an insight you have as to how you can "break away to commit," e.g., "Whenever I begin to procrastinate, I will break the task into one hour segments and complete the first hour that day."

Stage II: Awaiting Good Indicators

To help you harness the energy released by conviction and commitmen, we present the next **power thinking** strategy for decision making: *awaiting good indicators.*

THINKING AID 11
COMMITMENT COUNTERACTS INDECISION

- When I commit, the work becomes easier.

- I use **Thinking Tool G** when I need to make a commitment.

THINKING TOOL G
OBSTACLES TO COMMITMENT CHECKLIST

Read the following list and reflect upon the **power thinking** strategy you can use in the future to make more positive commitments. If one of the following behaviors applies to you, write today's date in the blank that precedes it and complete the sentence.

_____ **1. I start by procrastinating because I'm confused or overwhelmed.** In the future when I need to overcome procrastination, I will "break away to commit" by:

_____

_____

_____ **2. I have a tendency to exhibit ambivalence instead of speaking up to advance the welfare of others or myself.** In the future when I want to speak up, I will "break away to commit" by:

_____

_____

_____ **3. I tend to talk negatively about myself, to berate myself.** In the future when this behavior surfaces, I will "break away to commit" by:

_____

_____

_____ **4. I tend to minimize my abilities to take positive actions because I feel I must "wait for something to turn up."** In the future when I say this to myself, I will "break away to commit" by:

_____

_____

THINKING TOOL G (CONTINUED)

_____ 5. I tend to be impulsive, and/or I sometimes limit my follow-through. In the future when this behavior begins, I will "break away to commit" by:

_____

_____

_____ 6. I defer decisions to others, then later blame them or become angry because they did not execute the plan as I would have. In the future when this deference begins, I will "break away to commit" by:

_____

_____

_____ 7. I tend to go against the grain unnecessarily. I allow someone else to take a stand and then take the opposite position before I've really decided that this alternative position is correct. In the future when I do this, I will "break away to commit" by:

_____

_____

_____ 8. I tend to straddle the fence by saying how both sides of an issue sound good, so that neither I nor others really know who I am and where I stand. In the future, when I am tempted to hedge, I will "break away to commit" by:

_____

_____

✍ Think of a recent decision that you are implementing now. Does the work related to that decision inspire you?

____ yes   ____ sometimes ____ no

✍ Are you being challenged and made more knowledgeable through your involvement in this goal?

____ a lot   ____ about average ____ not very much

If your answers were "yes" and "a lot," you are using your inspiration in decision making. We commend you and your present decision-making abilities! If these were not your answers, you may enhance your decisions in two ways.

✍ First, identify a past decision that worked out well for you. It will be helpful if this decision was one in which you were in charge of the tasks to implement it. Analyze and write the qualities in the tasks that inspired you:

_____

If this quality did not come instantly to mind, these examples may help: Was it the interaction with new people that inspired you most? Solving a difficult problem and watching others (or yourself) prosper? Causing others to think in new ways or to understand new cause/effect relationships? Creating something new to help others? Gaining recognition, appreciation, or rewards for hard work that not everyone could have done? Assisting yourself and/or leading others to reach a positive purpose?

In essence, to create the energy you need to implement decisions, incorporate those personal, motivational qualities you identified into the decisions you have power to implement.

Example: One of us is inspired by appreciation from others. Knowing this, when we make decisions we include people who will appreciate our efforts. Doing so increases our energy as well as the quality of our work.

Similarly, you may find that your commitment and conviction increase when you become personally involved in fighting injustices. When these values are engaged, your commitment about the decision increases, as does your **power thinking**. Therefore, when you have to engage in tasks that result from decisions you did not make, and when you feel unmotivated to improve yourself, create a way to simultaneously add positive purpose for others. Alternatively, when you are not inspired by assisting others, use your insight to generate ways that the actions will concurrently benefit yourself.

☞ Second: To practice, think of a project you do not want to do that has been scheduled for the coming week. *Break away* for a moment to think about its tasks. *Commit* to them by adding something that motivates you or something that enhances what you want to achieve for yourself.

Before you read the next paragraph, pause for a moment and write that addition here:

_____

_____

If you wrote something in this blank that you truly value, you will notice an elevation in your emotional state. This is the feeling you are striving to achieve in all decisions before you take action. By awaiting these indicators, you can more easily move into a flow experience relative to that decision. When this state does not exist, you should use the **power thinking** strategy of administering *Proactive Repair*, or *PR*, which we describe next.

Stage III: Administer PR (Proactive Repair)

When decisions are not moving toward positive ends, flow experiences will not begin, and PR (Proactive Repair) should. *Proactive Repair* is defined as actions you take to correct mistakes in the decisions you advocated or tried to put in place. Proactive Repair contains two parts:

P = ***Proaction*** means to (1) find out what went wrong, (2) apologize for harms that the poor implementation of the decision incurred, (3) explain why you made the decision and why it did not achieve the results expected, and (4) state what you want to achieve in the future. If these actions and apologies are received with cooperation, you can make a new decision with DOUBLE THINKING (**Thinking Tool D**), the Weighted Characteristics Test (**Thinking Tool E**), *replacing excuses with explanations*, *breaking away to commit*, and *awaiting your good indicators*. Conversely, if your proaction is met with resistance, you can immediately administer *R = Repair*.

R = ***Repair*** means to take thoughtful action to remedy an existing negative situation. Correct as much damage as you can by following the negative response you received with a positive action, to ensure that the person who harbors ill feelings is left knowing you at your best. You do this by acknowledging the damage that you may have done to the other person and asking him or her for a suggestion as to how you can avoid such damages in the future.

We encourage you to not overlook the benefits of Proactive Repair, even in the seemingly smallest of decisions gone awry.

Example: During the first meeting of a national committee, Cathy and the other member from Texas disagreed upon a point. Cathy stated the reasons for her decision, but the other person did not. His anger demonstrated that he did not appreciate the challenge presented to his decision. Rather than allow this person to harbor ill feelings, or to establish an impression of her that did not match her own self-image, Cathy spent a portion of the evening following that exchange thinking of Proactive Repair actions. The next morning she greeted the man, and explained that her previous comments were not intended to dispute his words but rather to expand upon them. She also stated that she had not phrased her comments as well as she wished, and that she wanted to maintain the colleagueship they had prior to her remarks. The man was flattered that she took the time to explain her actions, and appreciated being valued as a person. The tension between them ceased. The alternative would have been to decide to do nothing and let the tension remain, which could have negatively affected that day's meeting.

The power in relationships that Proactive Repair creates — for you and for others — is important. We realize that it is difficult to do things for the first time. We want to assist you in thinking about these actions by asking you to practice Proactive Repair *now*.

✍ Think of a situation in which a decision you made may have inadvertently caused a difficulty for another person. Recreate that event in your mind; then write Proactive Repair actions and statements you could use to correct the negative results of that decision, similar to the actions that occurred between Cathy and her colleague.

_____

_____

_____

Now, at what time and place will you give this Proactive Repair statement to that person?

_____

In summary: Insight in decision making requires:

- breaking away to develop commitment and conviction,

- increasing emotional energy by awaiting indicators that you have indeed made a good decision, and

- *P*roactive *R*epair to overcome unforeseen negative outcomes.

SELF-KNOWLEDGE DURING DECISION MAKING

Stage I: Overcoming Negative Tendencies of Human Nature

The purpose of this section is to describe aspects of human nature that negatively influence decision-making:

- judging things as either "black or white,"
- doing things we like to do before those we don't,
- postponing large decisions, and
- doing what is *urgent* before what is *important* (and doing minor things before more difficult ones).

In the next few pages, you will read about the negative effects of these tendencies. If some are present in your personality, please write today's date in the blank that precedes that description. That way, you can reference this book in the future to measure the progress you have made since today in overcoming these negative tendencies. After each description, pause to relate the information to your life, and write an insight or action you can take in the future to circumvent the negative impact of this tendency.

✍ Last, before you read, it will be valuable to pause for a moment and think about a difficult decision you are facing at this point in your life. The larger and more important that decision is, the more fruitful the following reading will become. Write this decision down now:

_____

Which of the following qualities in your disposition can be circumvented to increase the quality of your decisions?

_____ 1. Do you want things to be either "black or white"? If you do, you may be unintentionally *minimizing the complexities of issues*. This decreases the long-term efficacy of your decisions, because variables in the decision can have ripple effects. What you perceive as the boundaries of a factor's significance are not the limits of its real impact. Thus, when you make a decision by merely saying "this is this" and "that is that," complexities inherent in the interactions of the steps of the action plan are not accounted for and will derail success during the implementation process. To avoid this outcome, we suggest that you weigh the talents, motives, and needs of others involved in that decision on the Weighted Characteristics Test before you make a decision.

Also, refer to "Mother Nature" as a reminder of your goal to overcome "black and white" thinking. As you may have already observed, Mother Nature can sensitize us to the intricacy of life. Every natural creation serves multiple purposes: you are not just a man, but a business leader, a friend, and a colleague; clouds provide shade, beauty, and rain; trees provide food, erosion protection, and lumber; and so on. So, too, will your decisions serve more than one purpose and create multiple changes in present realities.

_____ 2. Have others told you that you stereotype people, places, and events? Or do you find yourself saying "no" when asked to repeat an experience because you are convinced that it will be "just like the one before?" Or do you *not* "try again" if displeased with the results of a first attempt? If so, *stereotypic thinking* may be limiting the success of your decisions. Overcoming the tendency to stereotype is difficult because human nature tries to complete ideas by fitting them into familiar patterns, or *gestalts* (simple, global concepts), as rapidly as possible. To control stereotypic thinking, frequently ask yourself: "How is this incident different from those that precede it?" By doing so regularly, you build this important question into your habitual process of reasoning about decisions. It also encourages flexible interpretations of incoming information.

_____ 3. Do you finish tasks and make decisions that you like before those that you do not like? Do you make decisions that you know how to make faster and easier than those you do not?

To overcome this tendency, you need to gather the very best tools so *the best resources are readily available* at the moment a difficult and/or unpleasant decision is needed. For example, only a very small and simple change, like using the newest type of computer program to process the information relative to a difficult decision, will make it more appealing and less likely to be put off. Similarly, the **power thinking** tools in this chapter make decision-making easier.

✍ What tool can you use to make a present difficult decision easier?

_____.

✍ What is one easy thing you can do right now to prime the pump and get this big decision going? For example, power thinkers realize that a major decision has to be made at the end of the month, so they field-test a few of their ideas and begin Step 1 in Reasoning (**STOP** to collect information) immediately. They also begin a page on which to jot all of their ideas. What can you do right now about your difficult decision?

_____.

_____ 4. Do you do things that are urgent before those that are important? Do you often attend to the object, person, or problem that makes the most noise? Because we tend to do scheduled activities before nonscheduled ones, and more specific tasks before global ones, *making appointments with themselves* is how power thinkers allocate time to perform important tasks, such as creating visions for the future.

✍ How can you overcome indecision that arises because you have not scheduled time to make an important decision, or because the decision is too vague?

_____

In summary: Developing strategies to overcome negative effects of human tendencies will increase **power thinking** and the quality of decisions.

THINKING AID 12: OVERCOMING HUMAN NATURE REDUCES INDECISIVENESS

- Refrain from judging things as "black or white."
- Don't do things I like before things I don't like to do.
- Don't postpone large decisions.
- Don't let small crises get in the way of accomplishing what is important.

Thinking Aid 12 (on the facing page) is designed to remind you of these strategies.

Power thinkers use the Weighted Characteristics Test (**Thinking Tool E**) to consider the complexities that the talents, motives, and needs of others lend to decisions. They habitually ask, "How is this incident different from those that precede it?", use the best tools, and make appointments with themselves to have time to use the **power thinking** tools described so far in this book.

Stage II: Saying Yes And No Appropriately

When you are as capable of declining as of accepting invitations, your decision-making improves. Without this ability, you will continuously assume responsibilities that do not build **power thinking**, for overcommitment:

> ... is like a circle in the water
> Which never ceaseth to enlarge itself,
> Till by broad spreading it disperses to nought.
> — Shakespeare, *Henry V*

To develop the ability to say *yes* and *no* effectively, you should say *yes* to tasks that stretch your abilities or actualize the ideals of what you want in life, and say *no* to those that do not.

The most important strategy for accomplishing this is learning to identify *why you want* to say *yes* before you reflexively respond. To develop this habit, practice answering requests with a sentence that begins: "The reason I want to say *yes* (or *no*) is because _____." When this statement becomes habitual, you will less likely respond impulsively to the emotion of the moment.

✍ To practice this strategy, think of a person to whom (or a situation in which) it is difficult for you to say *no*. Write that person's (or situation's) name and why you have difficulty

saying *no* to that person, or describe the conditions that surround a particular situation and the values that lead you to
frequently say *yes* instead of *no*.

_____

_____

_____

To reduce your susceptibility in these situations, look at the value
statements listed below. While these qualities characterize everyone to some degree, power thinkers know how to *balance* these
values in their decisions — a skill the following discussion is designed
to help you develop. Saying *no* appropriately requires a psychological understanding of your basic personality needs and values.

✍ Which of the following reasons best explain why you do *not*
respond as you truly feel to the individual or situation you
wrote above? Place a "1" before the value that best describes
you, and a "2" beside the statement that describes you the
second best.

_____ A. The needs of others are more important than my own.

_____ B. I say *yes* to the majority of the requests made of me.

_____ C. The majority of the time I would rather work on a
team than alone.

_____ D. When I have made a commitment that is more taxing
than I had anticipated, I stick to it regardless of the cost.

Now, reread the statements you marked and find the discussion of each one below. (You may wish to read only these two
discussions and omit the others, which will not be as appli-
cable to you.) The next pages will explore some reasons why
saying *no* is so difficult, and reveal the **power thinking** strategies that enable you to decline unnecessary commitments.

A. The needs of others are more important than your own. Aren't
the priorities that you establish for yourself just as important
as those that others persuade you to value?

You can increase your decision-making power by placing priority upon actions that contribute to *your* growth and happiness. One way to do so is to do something for yourself every day. Bettering yourself helps you formulate higher-quality thoughts and decisions to share with others. Your self-reliance will increase, as you will not expect others to meet as many of your own needs. Giving more time and resources to yourself also increases the amount you are capable of achieving and sharing because you are not saying *yes* to too many inappropriate requests.

In addition, saying "no" in such situations also helps others identify **power thinking** abilities within *themselves* that can solve problems. If another person wants you to do something that he or she needs to do personally, saying *no* enables that person to take charge of his or her own problem. When you say *yes* and take action to alleviate another person's anxiety, you delay his or her identification of the cause of the problem. Furthermore, through naive actions based on your limited experience, you might create complications that actually increase the problem.

In reality, there is only one response you should give to friends and colleagues when they face difficulties: You can sincerely listen and question people to help them discover their own reasons, insights and self-knowledge. (Alternatively, you can give advice — but this advice, if unrequested, is likely to be based on *your* personality, circumstances, and self-knowledge.) The moment you cross the line from *listening* to *acting or deciding for* the person, you have said *yes* inappropriately and diminished that person's potential for growth.

If this pattern recurs frequently, evaluate requests by asking yourself: "Does this request fall within the context of my normal responsibilities? If not, do I have the *unique* resources and talents to meet this person's need?" Saying yes or no *selectively* allows you to focus your energies within your areas of talent — improving your results, your efficiency, and the total contribution your **power thinking** makes to others. To say *no* in such situations, use some or all of the following actions and **power thinking** strategies:

1. Refer the person to someone else, or explain why you feel you are not the best person to meet the request.

2. When someone makes a request, think to yourself, "Others will determine priorities for me if I don't have my own."

3. Have in mind one important objective you want to accomplish each day. In this way, when requests are made, you can respond by telling the person(s) that this objective is a priority that preceded their request.

4. Ask yourself: "Have I helped others or myself overcome this problem before?" If so, it should take limited time and be easy to do, and *yes* can be the correct answer.

5. Ask yourself: "Is this person a significant other in my life?" If so, you will receive an extra reward from saying *yes*, because by strengthening this person you also strengthen yourself.

B. *You say yes to the majority of the requests made of you.* It is likely that you are saying *yes* so frequently because you do not **STOP, CAUTION,** and **CAP** your reasoning enough before you answer. Any request should have a 50% chance of receiving a *no* from you. The following strategies will help you reason more powerfully and stop pursuing every direction that beckons.

1. Study how power thinkers commit to high-level priorities. Discuss with people you admire how they develop and maintain strong convictions and say *no* to lesser priorities.

2. If you want to say *no* but feel you can't, stop for a few seconds and say nothing, even silently counting to ten before saying *yes*. When you do this, other power thinkers may realize that you are hesitant, and they will help you to decline. They realize that it would not be in your own best interest to say *yes*.

3. If you cannot identify reasons for saying *yes*, you may be doing it to satisfy your ego needs, or because you assume

that your generosity will gain others' respect. A test for these possibilities is to ask yourself whether you sometimes feel "used" by others, and/or that others do not reciprocate in ways you desire. If you suspect this could be the case, analyze your actions to determine if your self-sacrificing and impulsiveness cause you to promise unrealistic performances. If you take on so many responsibilities that you are unable to deliver on your promises, others may subsequently judge you to be untrustworthy — losing you the very respect which was the reward you said *yes* to receive.

C. *The majority of the time you would rather work on a team than alone.* As you are aware, group work is best for many tasks. However, some people say *yes* to requests of others *merely to avoid being alone.* The problem of being in groups too often is that you lose the incentive and the time to develop your own unique talents and ideas. Also, you could become so much of a "groupie" that you lose sight of who you are, as the group limits opportunities to experience different aspects of yourself and life.

Instead, when you no longer say *yes* to others' every request, you will cease to be the first person that comes to mind for every undesirable job that "no one else will do." By becoming more decisive, you will project an image of someone who has many interests and commitments, and attract more people who assume their own responsibility.

You may be surprised to know that power thinkers spend more than 50% of their time alone, and that most of their close interactions involve only a few people. Thus, to make more effective decisions, set a goal each week to work by yourself or with one other person to develop a new idea, project or activity. Also, this change will increase your self-confidence.

D. *When you have made a commitment that is more taxing than you had anticipated, you stick to it no matter what the cost.* No one can perfectly judge the amount of time and effort some tasks take, even though experience at doing the same task may increase your accuracy at estimation. The following strategies can rescue you when a task proves to be more taxing than originally planned.

1. Ask others for help.

2. Ask for extensions of time.

3. Use the ADAPT method presented in Chapter 6 (pp. 180–83) and change the procedure in order to complete the task.

4. Share the completed portions with the people to whom you gave your commitment, and ask them to suggest what could be done to meet the deadline.

In summary: The second set of strategies to increase the power of self-knowledge during decision-making is to say *no* effectively:

- Value your own needs as highly as the needs of others.

- Do not automatically say *yes* to every request made of you.

- Enjoy working alone.

- Ask for suggestions to complete tasks that are more taxing than you had anticipated.

   Thinking Aid 13 (on the facing page) has been designed as a reminder of strategies for saying *no* effectively.

Stage III: Monitoring Self-Respect

Monitoring how much your self-respect rises and falls after each decision can become an effective gauge of the degree to which you are employing **power thinking** when others make requests of your resources and time.

You will know you have used **power thinking** during decision-making if your self-respect rises when the decision is made. For example, when you have made a good decision, regardless of the self-sacrifice required or difficulty of the task attempted, you

THINKING AID 13
SAY "NO" EFFECTIVELY

- My own needs are as important as the needs of others.

- I say no to requests that lie far outside my expertise.

- I enjoy working alone as well as on a team.

- I call upon other internal and external resources when tasks are more taxing than I originally estimated.

will experience *satisfaction*, *drive* and *enthusiasm* (Levels 4 through 6 on the emotional scale) and feel a sense of *pride* as you engage in the task. When you exercise the courage to explain your decision without excuses, you will also feel:

- a sense of personal gain,
- increased integrity, and
- free to focus upon more important decisions.

Conversely, if you do not use **power thinking** and say *yes* or *no* inappropriately, you will:

- sense a decrease in your self-respect,
- experience negative emotions, and/or
- become angry with the situation and be tempted to do less than your best or "beg off" by creating an excuse.

Because we all respond inappropriately at times, power thinkers learn to attend to their sense of self-respect by administering *PR* as soon as it indicates that a decision is not good. They also realize that as their self-respect increases and comfort zones rise, past decisions can be altered to accommodate their growth.

CONCLUSION

Self-knowledge contributes to **power thinking** during decision making when you:

- anticipate and eliminate negative tendencies of human nature;
- improve your ability to say *yes* and *no* appropriately, and
- use your self-respect as a measure of the merits of your decisions.

We realize that some strategies in this chapter may be difficult to master. The first attempt to overcome a personal deficit can become so frustrating that we give up.

Example: How vividly one of us recalls 20 years ago when the book *When I Say No I Feel Guilty* was published. Eager to improve in this area, we pounced into the first chapter. After the third page, the words were so vital to our improvement, but so hard to read!! By page four, however, anger began, and the book was closed with indignation. Such facts "*could not* be true about *me*!" Only three weeks later, through the use of **power thinking** strategies, did we return to the book and profit from its wisdom.

This story is shared in the event that something we say in this book provokes your strong negative emotions or a refusal to engage in the recommended activity. We encourage you to reassess your decision later.

The diagram in **Figure 4-2** shows the three reasons why decisions — even if they are successful — may be less than powerful. This diagram can also be used to assess which decision-making strategies will add the most immediate power to your own decision-making abilities.

1. In oval A , if you presently make decisions that are not as effective as you want, but you truly cannot identify the

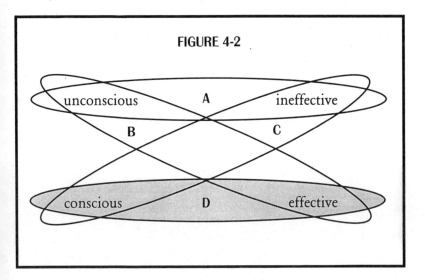

FIGURE 4-2

reasons for their ineffectiveness, strategies to strengthen your basic reasoning abilities will be valuable — such as DOUBLE THINKING, the Weighted Characteristics Scale, and eliminating excuses.

2. In oval B, if you succeed at times but are not really sure why some decisions work better than others, strategies that strengthen self-knowledge are needed — such as overcoming negative tendencies of human nature, saying *yes* and *no* more effectively, and monitoring your self-respect.

3. In oval C, if you are reasoning well but your decisions are less successful than you desire, we recommend that you master strategies that strengthen your insight — such as asking more questions, building stronger commitment, adding personal motivators, awaiting good indicators before making a decision, and using PR (Proactive Repair).

If you are aware of the reasons why your decisions are good and know that they result from creative **power thinking**, as depicted in oval D, then the strategies in Chapters 5 and 6 will add to your repertoire.

Before you leave this chapter, it will be profitable for you to review the nine strategies for powerful decision-making by recalling their names. Can you list them on the next page? If you cannot recall one, return briefly to the pages indicated to reaffirm its title. In this way, you will remember the information from this chapter more accurately and with less effort.

The strategies for improved decision making are:

REASONING: 1. _____
(pages 73-90)
                      2. _____

                      3. _____

INSIGHT: 4. _____
(pages 90-99)
                      5. _____

                      6. _____

SELF-KNOWLEDGE: 7. _____
(pages 99-110)
                      8. _____

                      9. _____

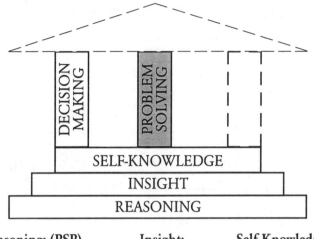

Reasoning: (PSP)	Insight:	Self-Knowledge:
STOP: read/reflect/write	Break Away	Talents/Needs/Motives
P = PROBING FOR BEST	*INTERNAL PROBLEM-*	*GOOD ADVICE*
PATTERN	*SOLVING SPACE*	
CAUTION: listen/ask questions	High Spirits	Analyze Beliefs
S = SELECT STRATEGY	*UP INSTEAD OF OUT OR*	*ABOUT SUCCESS AND*
	IN	*FAILURE*
GO: CAPped Speech	Create Flow	Strong Self-Concept
P = PROACTIVELY	*VISION VS. DAYDREAMS*	*SELF-RESILIENCY*

CHAPTER 5
Power Thinking and Problem Solving

Powerful problem solving overcomes challenges by first identifying cognitive reasons, subconscious insights, and personality-related influences on difficulties in the problem, and then actively working to bring them into some positive solution. In turn, sturdy reasoning leads to the recognition of the patterns that generated a dilemma, and the proactive innovations that can solve it.

Similarly, insight contributes to problem solving by (1) overcoming negative emotions that arise when challenges occur, and (2) finding the initial intention that engaged an obstacle. Your insight will verify if you are correct in a problematic situation, however strongly others contend that you are not. Perhaps your underlying intention that led to the difficulty was good. However, without strong insight, it becomes easy to overlook your good intention and listen to negative emotions — which often demand that you do the opposite of what would be productive.

Example: Suppose your underlying intent in an interaction with a friend was to offer assistance. Your friend misunderstood your intent and became angry and defensive. Without strong insight, your natural reflex would likely be to withdraw. This action would fulfill the exact opposite of your positive intent: not only failing to apply your talents to your friend's problem, but creating a new difficulty between your friend and you. Insight inspires you to defuse your friend's hurt feelings and focus attention back on the original problem.

Likewise, self-knowledge contributes to problem solving in that it strengthens your sense of your own ability to overcome adversity. Such resiliency is necessary in problem solving, especially before success becomes imminent and when perseverance is most arduous. Also, when two people conflict, the initial point of disagreement is not alone in fueling the problem. Personality-related variables intertwine to determine how much each person needs to exercise control of the situation. The more skillful you become at personal assessment, the more ably you can address these multiple, interactive causes.

By analyzing your beliefs about success and failure, you can remove unintentional, self-imposed barriers that will inhibit your success in problem solving.

To begin, first describe an important personal or professional challenge you recently solved, then indicate what you did to solve it:

Problem:_____

_____

_____

_____

_____

Solution:_____

_____

_____

_____

_____

_____

_____

With this experience in mind, we want you to complete **Thinking Tool H,** which will help you become aware of your beliefs about your own past successes and failures. In the blank that precedes each statement, place a check mark if the sentence is true for you. At the end of the list, you will use these markings to discover information about the effect of your beliefs upon your problem-solving success.

THINKING TOOL H

ANALYZING BELIEFS ABOUT SUCCESS AND FAILURE

____ 1. In your life, fewer successes have occurred through luck, politics, inequitable standards, or injustices than through sustained effort.

____ 2. In your life, success is not accidental.

____ 3. A strong belief in your own abilities was an important component in past successes.

____ 4. When you experience success, it creates more positives for you and saves you time, rather than increasing your demands. It saves time because it eliminates the need for repeated trials to reach the same goal.

____ 5. For you, past successes have led to increased quality in your life.

____ 6. To be most successful, you have to love what you do.

____ 7. When you were successful, it was because you found your niche, and you can describe the special flair you contribute to that niche.

____ 8. When you were successful, you used a strategy to assure yourself that you would not accept failure.

____ 9. For you, success provides energy for new challenges rather than stress and increased pressure.

____ 10. You view success as running a race between yourself and your ever-increasing ability to exceed your last level of performance, rather than winning a race between yourself and others.

____ 11. When you succeeded in the past, you expected the result to culminate in greater responsibility for developing better ideas and interacting with more challenging goals.

THINKING TOOL H (CONTINUED)

___ 12. You have found that your success stirred up anger or envy in others. You realized that this "bad blood" existed and took action to channel it into positive directions.

___ 13. You found that to be successful you had to become more capable and/or had to work harder than other people. As a result, some people became jealous. Therefore, success has taught you to forgive and forbear jealousy.

___ 14. When you succeed, you do not experience an increased fear that future goals will end in failure. You are not afraid that you will be found out; that you do not know all that you are expected to know for this new level of accomplishment. You do not became concerned that you will be found capable of "talking the talk but not walking the walk." You can describe the strategy you use to avoid this fear.

___ 15. In past successes, you knew that you had not "reached your level of incompetence," so even if success brought demands for which you had no previous experience, you never became so scared that you did not want to try again.

___ 16. For you, success is not measured by the critiques or compliments of others but by how successful you feel at this moment in time.

___ 17. You have noticed that neither succeeding nor failing causes you to become less sensitive to others, withdraw into your own goals or overextend your ego. You can describe the strategies you use to not treat others differently whether you succeed or fail.

___ 18. Past successes increased your self-reliance.

THINKING TOOL H (CONTINUED)

____ 19. It is important to you to try many things to become successful because doing so enables you to throw away the trials that do not meet your standards.

____ 20. You believe *you* are in control of the level of success you will achieve.

____ 21. You agree that high-achieving people fail from time to time but that failing does not stop them from pursuing and achieving monumental victories.

____ 22. After failing, more so than after successes, you fulfill your need for introspection.

____ 23. Your failures have taught you how to adapt.

____ 24. Failures have caused you to acknowledge your mistakes and learn from them. Without your failures, you would have invested more energy in trying to disavow your mistakes.

____ 25. In your life, most failures occurred because you worked too fast, left something lacking or insufficient; or neglected to do something you did not know how to do.

____ 26. Past failures often increased your fear of failure or made you apathetic.

____ 27. In your experiences, you found that one of the costs of failure is the loss of opportunities. Failing causes you to return to the same goal rather than enabling you to move to another goal, as successes allow you to do.

____ 28. Failures leave an empty place in your heart.

____ 29. When you fail, only after awhile can you permit the full gamut of emotions to be experienced again, but you do open yourself totally to feeling all emotions again, regardless of how painful they may be.

THINKING TOOL H (CONTINUED)

_____ 30. Failures have increased your ability to trust the right people.

_____ 31. Your failures have come from errors that led to a loss of control or a negative momentum. When these errors occurred, you chose to continue to work toward a satisfactory result, abandon effort, concede, or ante up.

_____ 32. Failures helped you learn about success because you can now better pinpoint what can be improved to obtain even greater success in projects.

_____ 33. You believe that when you take things head-on there is always a chance that you may fail, but that doing so is better than stagnating on the sidelines.

_____ 34. Failures increased your self-knowledge so similar defeats did not reoccur.

_____ 35. One of the outcomes of past failures was that you re-examined yourself in exquisite detail and set higher principles so you would never allow yourself to be knocked down again.

_____ 36. Knowing that you survived a failure, even made something fruitful of it, has increased your risk-taking.

_____ 37. Your failures were humbling and increased the value you place upon courage in yourself and others.

_____ 38. You believe failures are temporary.

_____ 39. Failures made you resilient to being "spooked by life" and reduced your vulnerability.

_____ 40. Failures have been useful experiences for you. They increased your determination and made you search for new methods of operating.

_____ 41. Failures enabled you to establish the conviction that accidents will never govern your life.

To analyze if your beliefs about success and failure have limited your problem-solving abilities, we want you to know that the most successful and powerful problem solvers in the world believe that *all of the statements are true!* Thus, by rereading the statements you disagreed with, you can discover where your beliefs are specifically limiting your success.

Items 1-10 are statements about the positive outcomes of success. Any item in numbers 1-10 that are not marked with a check indicate that your beliefs about the *value of success* are not as strong as those of more successful power thinkers. Specifically, the expectations you hold for your own capabilities may be too low, which restricts problem-solving success. Reread each item you did not check to identify why you do not believe the statement to be true in your life, and turn back to **Thinking Aid 6: Evaluate Your Beliefs** (p. 57) to analyze the negative consequences of the belief.

Items 11-20 describe negative qualities of success that, if left unattended, can diminish the positive outcomes of your decisions. If any items between 11-20 are not checked, your beliefs about that item and the demands success places upon you are not as strong as those of power thinkers. These beliefs can suggest reasons why you "clutch" at the doorstep of potential success, as you may believe (consciously or subconsciously) that you cannot handle the negative effects and increased responsibility that success generates. As you reread each item not checked, analyze why you do not find that item true in your life, using **Thinking Aid 6** (p. 57). By doing so, you can change your beliefs to better reflect the values that are most important to you. Select one of the 13 **Thinking Aids** and 8 **Thinking Tools** described so far in this book to employ when obstructions to success arise.

Items 21-29 describe the negative consequences of failure. If you left any items from 21-29 unchecked, this suggests that you lack confidence in your ability to solve problems. As a result, you may pretend to — or actually — lose interest in areas of your life where you encounter problems. You may also have a high sensitivity to criticism and avoid exploring new ideas. If any item within numbers 21-29 are not checked, you have probably suffered so much from past failure(s) that you need new strategies before you can risk failing again. You can become a more powerful thinker by using this chapter's strategies to overcome these and other thought patterns that lead to a loss of control in the face of challenges. Again, as you reread items not checked, analyze why you do not believe that item to be true in your life. Those who have used **Thinking Aid 6** (p. 57) to complete this analysis found they could select new **power thinking** strategies to obtain more value from failures in the future.

Items 30-41 describe benefits that can result from failures. Any unchecked item suggests a belief that is keeping you from maximizing the potential for growth that failure affords. As you reread each item not checked, analyze why you do not believe that item to be true in your life. Those who have used **Thinking Aid 6** (p. 57) to complete this analysis found that they could select a **power thinking** strategy to employ in the future to obtain new growth when failure occurred.

In summary: **Power thinking** values and uses both success *and* failure for the contributions they make to stronger reasoning, insight, and self-knowledge. These will ultimately create progress and positive, productive outcomes, *regardless of whether the initial lessons were learned through success or failure*. The ability to grow *equally* from success and failure comes from analyzing inadequate prior beliefs and using the following strategies.

Realizing that reasoning, insight, and self-knowledge contribute equally to problem solving, we will now describe strategies for each that can increase your problem-solving success.

REASONING DURING PROBLEM SOLVING

Stage I: P=Planning

The important first step in solving a problem is deciding whether it is worth the effort to solve it. However, there is a trap of believing that problems will go away of their own accord. Even the smallest problem has a insistent personality! Problems do not like being ignored, and unless we give them the attention they deserve as soon as possible, they will go to extremes to get it. Therefore, like decision-making (Chapter 4) and personal change (Chapter 6), problem-solving demands that all dimensions of **power thinking** (reasoning, insight, and self-knowledge) be engaged simultaneously. This process is the **Problem-Solving Process (PSP)**.

The Problem-Solving Process (PSP) begins with **P = Probing** for a set of **S = Strategies** that interact **P = Proactively** — in advance of action — to reverse a negative pattern. To help you consider adversities from many perspectives simultaneously, we ask that you write all the information relative to a problem in a circle graphic, as in **Thinking Tool I** (on the next page).

✍ To use the **P = Planning** to unite all components of **power thinking**, recall a problem you now face. On the circle in **Thinking Tool I**, use two different colored pens. With one color, write the information you have to date in each section of the circle that relates to yourself. Then, with a second color, next to what you wrote about yourself, write what you know about others involved in the dilemma. When finished, read all your thoughts without pausing. Reread to identify interactions among problematic variables.

Using this comprehensive thinking pattern ensures that you will consider multiple tools in the solution. By contrast, without **Thinking Tool I**, human nature will initiate logic alone to attack the negative emotions that arise in difficulties. As we stated in previous chapters, emotions are *not* governed by logic — so reasoning alone cannot eliminate the negative impact of anger, hurt and fear in your subconscious. Here, because you are focused on finding

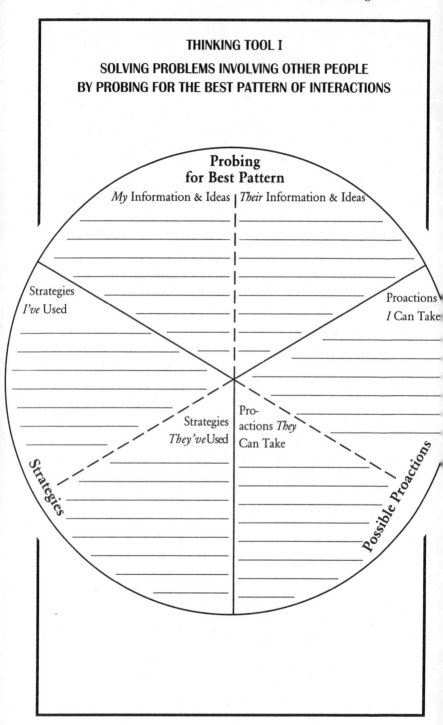

THINKING TOOL I
SOLVING PROBLEMS INVOLVING OTHER PEOPLE
BY PROBING FOR THE BEST PATTERN OF INTERACTIONS

**Probing
for Best Pattern**

My Information & Ideas | *Their* Information & Ideas

Strategies
I've Used

Proactions
I Can Take

Strategies
They've Used

Pro-
actions *They*
Can Take

Strategies

Possible Proactions

the interactions between variables, your negative emotions are not triggered when others focus on a single aspect of the problem that was your responsibility. Thus, the detrimental impact of those emotions upon your reasoning and self-knowledge is circumvented.

Finally, such comprehensive thinking reduces the temptation to jump on a pendulum and correct one excess with its opposite. Rarely does implementing the reverse of existing variables initiate a proactive plan for success.

Example: Airline X undercuts ticket prices so that their fares are lower than Airline Y's. If Airline Y attempts to reverse their position of being the higher-priced carrier so they become the lowest-priced carrier, the further reduced ticket price only compounds the airline industry's problems. This is why power thinkers in airline companies generally seek only to *meet* competitor prices.

In conclusion, the surest sign that you are creating a good solution, even when this solution is not yet visible, is that your confidence rises. It ascends because insight, reason, and self-knowledge have unified. As a result, insight is continuously seeking to solve the problem outside of your conscious awareness.

In summary: Planning involves the use of **power thinking** through reasoning, insight, and self-knowledge to:

- identify the interweaving of intentions, emotions, logic, and talents that create a problem, and

- move toward a positive action, either to create productive purposes or to circumvent a potential problematic situation before it becomes a crisis.

In the process, your confidence rises, as does your awareness of the multiple interactions that create problems. When you have reread your writings in the circle, you can more pow-

erfully *S*elect a strategy for solving this problem *P*roactively. We describe this *S*election
process next.

Stage II: S=Select The Best Strategy

In this section, you will learn to think powerfully about your
problem by selecting a procedure to channel your reasoning. We
have six problem-solving procedures that strengthen judgment
during problem solving. As we describe each procedure, have in
mind the problem you analyzed in Stage I (the preceding section).
When a procedure appeals to you relative to that problem, you
may be tempted to pause from reading and employ it mentally or
in writing. Please feel free to stop and do so. In the future, referencing **Thinking Aids 14-19** can engage this same selection and
self-initiation so your problem-solving deliberations become more
rapid.

☞ *Matrices.* Matrices are the best procedure to use when you
are confused about a problem. This procedure enables you to
identify different paths to a solution. Also, if your confidence has not risen or you need more time to think about
multiple interactive causes of a problem, matrices secure this
extra time for contemplation, because you have to take the
time to construct a chart. Using a matrix enables you to:

- "traverse the territory in many directions" and overcome
  preconceived viewpoints (as described on pp. 10–12),
- activate creativity, and
- search for alternatives that are unconstrained by your past
  experiences and outdated beliefs.

Many well-known leaders have employed matrices: for example, Lee Iacocca used them to conceive positive courses of
action for the Chrysler Corporation. **Thinking Aid 14** (on
the facing page) will help remind you of their usefulness.
    To use this procedure, sketch (or photocopy) a matrix like
the one in **Thinking Tool J**. Next, write all the attributes

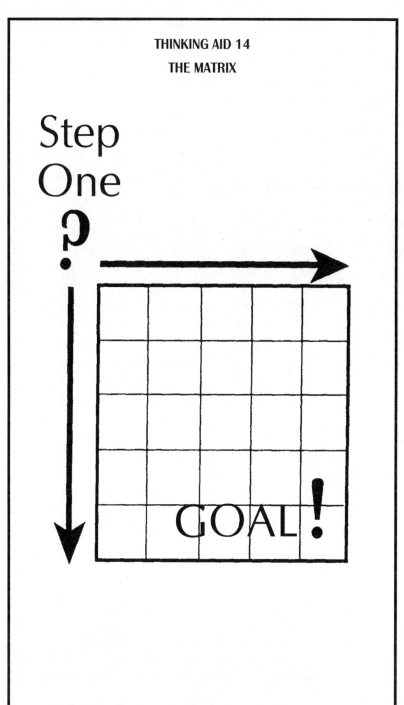

about one dimension of a problem along the top columns of the graph, and attributes of another dimension along the rows on the left side. Then, write the pluses and minuses from the interaction of variables in boxes within the grid.

Example: In Figure 5-1 (on the facing page), Lee Iacocca listed properties of the American economy — which influences people's abilities to purchase cars — across the top of his matrix, and properties of the automobile industry along the left. Inside the matrix, he then wrote actions which his company could take to capitalize on the interactions between each pair of factors. For instance, one property of the automobile industry is that it is *highly competitive*: the company that can make its products and prices most attractive will sell the most. One property of the economy is that *all people are affected by its strength*: when it is weak, people's buying power is reduced. Thus, Iacocca wrote that Chrysler might increase sales by offering customers a unique feature: instantly adjusting car loans to a lower interest rate if prevailing rates dropped at any time during a customer's loan period.

You may find that anticipating probable *benefits* is more difficult than predicting *deficits*. Without a matrix as a reasoning tool, we tend to overemphasize negative outcomes when reasoning. To be most successful, it is important to write in each square both positive *and* negative results of each interaction.

Example: Chester Carlson approached corporate executives from numerous companies with a new idea for copying documents, called a "copying machine." All but one CEO found faults with the quality of the images that the earliest machine produced. Xerox Corporation, however, looked beyond the poor images, and saw the multiple advantages of photocopying over carbon copying.

THINKING TOOL J
THE MATRIX FOR PROBLEM SOLVING

Dimension 1: _____

Interacting Factors					

Dimension 2: _____

FIGURE 5-1

IACOCCA'S MATRIX (COMPLETED)

Dimension 1: THE AMERICAN ECONOMY

		Fluctuating	Based on supply and GNP	Gaining or losing strength internationally	Influenced by many different sectors of society	All people depend on its strength
Dimension 2: THE AUTOMOBILE INDUSTRY	**Is highly competitive**	Make cars in a more varied price range	Find a new population to buy cars	Gain large market share in Canada	Incentives to Chrysler employees to buy Chrysler	Fluctuate loan payments based on inflation
	Employs a lot of people	Tenure guaranteed	Employees make things besides cars	Open dealerships internationally	Hire from all socio-economic levels	Barter with employees
	Touches each person's life	Planned carhood	Increase need for 3-car families	Increase need/value of 1-car families internationally	Make buses	Add entertainment features inside car
	Uses products from many other industries	Work on producing products cheaper	Buy our own steel and plastics companies	Find cheapest suppliers	Build new plants near cheapest suppliers	Diversify our suppliers to hedge for losses
	Is characterized by rapidly changing technology	Use technology that aids economy	Locate easy-to-operate technology	Best technology from most stable companies	Teach people how to use new technology in cars	Make instructions simple
	Is influenced by government	Federal auto laws change according to economy	Identify new markets that will improve GNP, be protected by govt. regulations	Purchase equipment in countries w/ strongest currency	Market to sectors of population working in government	Lobby to pass lower taxes on cars for people in low socio-economic levels
	Projections based on speculations of public demand	Make parts that can be interchange to update cars	Increase unique "want" factors built into our cars	Survey for needs of public in each nation	Make our high-profit cars more attractive to the public	Donate a % of every sale to a charity that people in America value

Similar negative thinking — because matrices were not used — occurred when Western Union turned down the rights to manufacture the telephone; when the president of Michigan Savings Bank advised against investments in the Ford Motor Company because the car was "only a fad" and the horse was here to stay; and when the president of 20th Century Fox decided against buying a television channel, stating that people would soon grow "tired of staring at a plywood box every night."

In summary: Use matrices at times when alternatives over-whelm you, your confidence wanes, or no solutions appear. Write variables that impact your problem along the two axes — e.g., factors under your control could be written across the top; those you don't control on the left. Then, as comprehensively as possible, write in each box of the chart the positive and negative interactions of the factors interacting there.

☞ *Backward reasoning* is the second problem-solving procedure. It is valuable when the solution is clear but the first step to achieve the goal is not. **Thinking Aid 15** is designed to help you remember this strategy. To begin backward reasoning, use **Thinking Tool K** (p. 133) and write the *solution* to your problematic situation at the top. Then, beneath that, list the step that would have to occur right before it. Continue to reason backward until you can write a step that you can take tomorrow to set this positive pattern in action.

Example: The chairman of the board of trustees of a major university unilaterally envisioned that the institution should increase enrollment by 20% each year for five years until its size had doubled. This chairman reasoned that such an increase would produce profits, just as a 20%-a-year increase in corporate size had done for

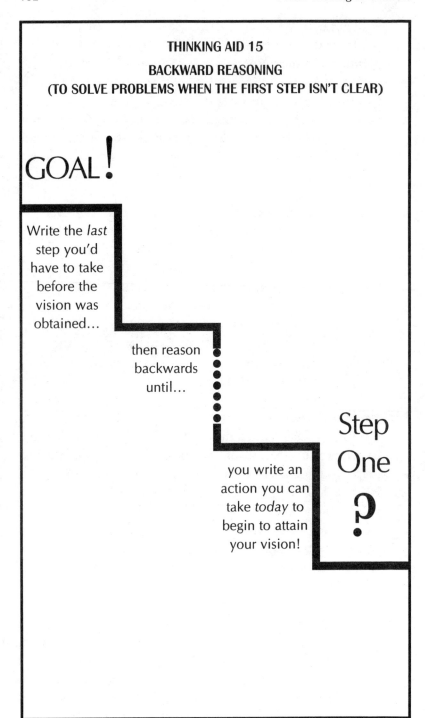

THINKING TOOL K

BACKWARD REASONING STEPS

VISION: _____

Step that will have to take place immediately before my vision can be attained: _____

Step before that: _____

Step before that: _____

Step before that: _____

Step before that: _____

Step before that: _____

Step before that: _____

Step before that: _____

Step before that: _____

Step before that: _____

Step before that: _____

Step before that: _____

Step before that: _____

Step I can take TODAY to start working toward attaining my vision: _____!

his optical products business. Fortunately, the president of that university used backward reasoning to demonstrate to the board how this solution would not be appropriate for a nonprofit organization like the university.

The president wrote at the top of his chart the goal *Doubling the size of the university within 5 years.* Then he wrote that for this goal to be reached, the university had only 60 months to: build nine new buildings; double the support staff; search for 70 new faculty members; develop new and unique curricula to attract a new population of students who were not presently attending this university; develop a plan to pay for these initiatives; hire people to develop this plan; appoint search committees to identify the people to hire to develop the plan; allow three months for this first committee to develop *their* plan, etc.

The president's backward reasoning prevented the university from acting upon an un-powerful solution which would have resulted in tremendous long-term damage to the university's reputation as well as to its fiscal health.

In brief, backward reasoning is the best strategy when you have clearly identified the solution you want but do not know how to begin toward that goal today. It can also help you analyze how effective a solution is likely to be.

☞ *Begin now but not at the core of the problem* is the best procedure to use when you are new to a specific knowledge domain and have not had very much experience with the positive pattern you want to set in motion in that field. **Thinking Aid 16** will help remind you of this strategy.

By beginning with simple tasks you do well, you can reach solutions more rapidly. Specifically, just as the cause for a densely knotted ball of yarn cannot be seen at the outset but will be only found at its core, the central issues of new and

THINKING AID 16: BEGIN NOW BUT NOT AT THE CORE OF THE PROBLEM

large challenges often become more visible only after the easier, external knots have been untied.

To *begin now but not at the core of the problem*, take an action to improve one aspect of the problem that is under your control. Then, analyze the effects of the action you took, and turn your thinking toward a second aspect of the challenging situation that is under your control. As you work to rectify these dimensions of the problem, the larger, more nebulous "problem solution" will emerge. One knot at a time, the problematic web unravels. Continuing to make minor corrections, so that your success at each small step is assured, means that these separate, less complicated dimensions of the situation will not become more entangled themselves. Also, your actions will make positive changes in the conceptual and behavioral patterns that support the central issue.

If, instead, you naively yank the ball of "intertwined causes" to establish an ill-conceived grand solution, knots will form. These knots intensify the problematic dimensions of the central issue, because people's feelings are hurt and damaging procedures have been set in motion. In turn, these actions encourage some people to swing far away from the actions you engage (the pendulum swing effect) or to dig in their heels and refuse to support any subsequent action you take (championing the status quo, and neutralizing their positive power to contribute to the solution, by protesting or becoming corporate "deadwood"). In summary, *beginning now but not at the core* enables you to identify opportunities that others have missed and to eliminate self-serving solutions.

The next three procedures assist you to move forward if you cannot think of *any* solution. These procedures are: *setting a deadline, making an assembly line,* and *channeling solutions into your talent areas.*

☞ *Set a deadline.* Whenever a problem "nags" you to work on it or when you feel guilty for not having solved it, a good procedure is to *establish a deadline*. Because deadlines establish a time in which a product will be delivered, you commit more rapidly and work more diligently toward success. You do so to save face, avoid disappointing others, and demonstrate your competence.

It is important for you to examine *your* response to deadlines, however, since some people do not respond well to the pressure that self-imposed deadlines create. To complete this self-analysis, recall a recent deadline that you set for yourself on a personal or professional task. On page 139, we ask you to list the positive and negative feelings/behaviors that occurred because you imposed this deadline on yourself or accepted it as a task.

Example: An insurance executive completed this self-analysis:

Positive Feelings And Behaviors

1. When I reach my deadline, I feel satisfied — as if a weight is lifted from my shoulders.
2. When I impose a deadline, I do higher quality work because I concentrate more, and I force myself to use my most intense, highest levels of thinking uninterrupted.
3. With a deadline, I stick to the task at hand instead of frequently changing my focus. This saves me the time of having to reorient myself to the task; my time is spent in advancing forward rather than merely trying to recapture former thoughts, so I accomplish more.
4. With a deadline, the results of my work are more timely.
5. When I set a deadline, I do not overkill an idea, as I tend to do when I allow myself unlimited time to work on something.

Negative Feelings And Behaviors

1. I do not eat healthy and I interrupt my sleeping schedule.
2. When I underestimate the time it will take to reach a deadline, I fall behind on other

THINKING AID 17
SET A DEADLINE

projects.

3. I have more difficulty engaging in reverie to strengthen my insight.

4. I need to improve my creative ability to maintain my important, normal routines and still meet deadlines without as much self-imposed pressure.

We ask you now to complete, in the space below, your analysis of how you respond to deadlines — your own or others'.

Positive Feelings And Responses

1. _____
2. _____
3. _____
4. _____
5. _____

Negative Feelings And Responses

1. _____
2. _____
3. _____
4. _____
5. _____

What insights did you gain about the value of deadlines for you?

_____
_____
_____

Now compare your answers to those of the insurance executive in our example. When he completed this analysis, he realized that his responses to deadlines were more positive than he had anticipated. He also discovered that in the future he wants to add the following **power thinking** strategies:

1. focus his priorities in areas of his talent;
2. take more frequent, but earned, breaks to maintain his daily routine;
3. say *no* to low-priority activities; and
4. channel solutions into his talent areas (pp. 142-144) so he can better enjoy the challenges that deadlines provide.

Before he completed this personal analysis, this executive believed that he worked best by establishing as few deadlines as possible. Now, he uses them frequently to attack problems, and he has fewer problems in his life as a result.

☞ *Make an assembly line.* The second procedure to guide reasoning when no solutions have yet been found is to make an assembly line. Using this procedure means you will *group similar or related aspects* of a problem, *complete an entire group of tasks* at one time, then *move consecutively to the next set* until you reach a solution. Doing so increases your efficiency because (a) you gradually refine your approach to each kind of task, and (b) you are less likely to overlook or forget elements of each task. This procedure can be especially useful when a problem involves several people, because when you approach each of them in turn, you can be sure to cover all the issues relating to that person at the same time. **Thinking Aid 18** (on the facing page) will help remind you of this strategy.

Example: One CEO said that when it came time to downsize his company, instead of completely eliminating a full division or a specific rank of employee, he used the assembly line procedure to guide his reasoning. He identified all the employees that would be affected by downsizing, and he proceeded to interview them one after another. As each interview ended, the next became more refined and valuable in pinpointing a solution. As a result, employee talents were rechanneled,

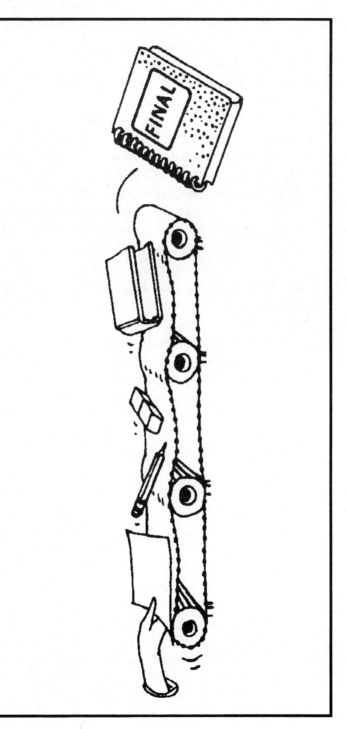

THINKING AID 18: MAKE AN ASSEMBLY LINE

and the company identified a unique niche in the market to pursue.

☞ *Channeling actions into your talent areas.* When a problem gets worse despite your actions, it is a signal that the plan you set in motion either does not match your talents or does not lead to the core of the problem. Therefore, you should alter your course of action by re-engaging in comprehensive thinking — doing a DOUBLE THINK with **Thinking Tool D** — to find a more appropriate solution.

In essence, this procedure entails reframing the demands of the problem so that you can attack it with your personal strengths. Since your talents are unique and powerful, using them to approach your problem will speed you toward a more successful solution. **Thinking Aid 19** (on the facing page) will help remind you of this possibility.

Example: Mike, a postal carrier whom we counseled, applied this procedure to remove a problem with his job. He had inherited a rural postal route that was the best in his area. Unfortunately, the route presented a problem. He enjoyed eating lunch with others, and the way the route had been mapped, he was not near any restaurants at midday.

After several days of eating alone, Mike decided to use one of his talents to solve his problem. He was the most skilled organizer of mail route planning. The other carriers had experienced also problems with the existing routes. Therefore, he approached his superior for permission to redesign his and other carriers' routes. His superior agreed to allow new routes to be drawn up, provided Mike could also address a problem the superior foresaw on the horizon: a new subdivision in their area was near completion, and no new postal carriers were going to be hired to accommodate this region.

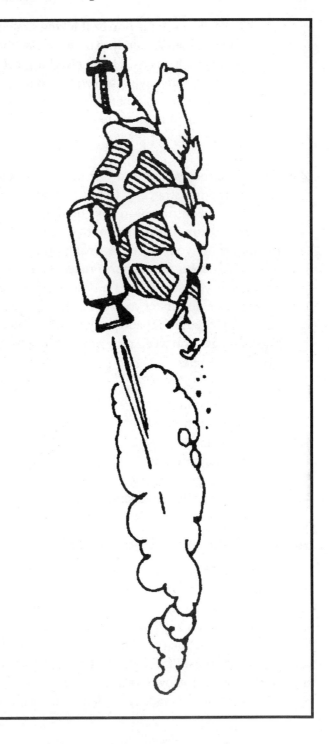

THINKING AID 19:   CHANNEL SOLUTIONS INTO YOUR TALENT AREAS

Mike used the **power thinking** strategies we taught and worked diligently to design a plan that would meet everyone's needs. He received a great deal of satisfaction from having solved his colleagues' problems, his superior's problem, *and* his own original problem — being able to eat lunch with his colleagues again as a result.

If you have not yet applied one of the previously discussed problem-solving strategies to your present situation, do so now, either in writing or in your head, employing one of the problem-solving procedures we have described. Don't worry about whether you chose the wrong procedure; if you have, you will discover its inappropriateness as you use it. (For instance, if you set yourself a deadline for aspects of problems that are not under your control, you'll eventually recognize this procedure's inadequacy.) We list the six procedures below and ask you to employ one now to experience its benefits for yourself.

1. Matrices
2. Backward reasoning
3. Begin now but not at the core
4. Set a deadline
5. Make an assembly line
6. Take actions in advance of problems by channeling activities into your talent and skill areas

Stage III: Speaking P=PROACTIVELY

Proactive **CAP**ped speech during problem solving means telling people the upside *and* the downside of a problem and its potential solutions. Our research indicates that people will commit steadfastly when told both the positives and negatives about problems and solutions. Such comments also ensure that they will not veto positive purposes through inaction. Specifically, when both sides of the issue are known, and reasons for moving ahead with a particular solution are made clear, determination rises. Moreover, people will remain loyal to that solution because they tend to judge it as positive, even if it does not prove to be as successful as they had hoped. Thus, the last reasoning strategy in PSP is to make sure your first written or oral expressions about a problem explain the positive *and* negative variables associated with the solution.

In summary: The reasoning strategies for problem solving can be remembered with the acronym **PSP** (*P*lanning positive patterns by employing *S*trategies *P*roactively).

INSIGHT DURING PROBLEM SOLVING

Stage I: Problem-Solving Space and Bracketing

To strengthen insight, engage *problem-solving space* and *bracketing*. These actions provide blocks of time to nurture insight, accomplish PSP, and write about your initial feelings and ideas. Even though you will probably never share these feelings and ideas with those involved in the problem, expressing them enables your subconscious to move forward.

☞ *Internal problem-solving space* is our term for psychologically engaging in an uninterruptible, distraction-free appointment with yourself. Entering your internal problem-solving space frequently will get you to rethink the things you dearly prize and set new standards for yourself.

☞ *External problem-solving space* is a portion of your home or office (even simply a specific chair) which you designate as a pondering area. Your physical movement to that location ensures that you enter your *internal* problem-solving space more efficiently.

☞ *Bracketing* is a method of entering your internal problem-solving space whenever the need arises, in addition to the time you regularly block off to do so. Specifically, whenever you experience a disappointment, your subconscious and rational mind has to feel its way through shock, disillusionment, and loss. This takes time, and *bracketing* helps you maintain perspective without rushing the thinking/healing process.

Bracketing is used each time your mind wanders to this disappointment while you are working on another priority. Engage *bracketing* as soon as your mind wanders from the task at hand: look at your watch and allow yourself one, five, or even fifteen minutes to think about the complication. Then promise yourself to return — and *do return* — to the task at hand when this period has elapsed. If the bracketed time was insufficient, set an appointment with yourself to enter your internal problem-solving space as soon as possible *after* the present priority has been completed.

Using bracketing in this way respects your insight's call to *break away*. It also places the problem in the pressure cooker of the subconscious for continuous refinement while your conscious activities return to the priority of the moment. Bracketing frees your mind to process a difficulty at its own pace and does not rush you into making rash decisions based on negative or confused feelings. Moreover, the bracketing period enables your mind to integrate new information you experienced during the day that is related to the problem. Similarly, by disciplining yourself to think about the problem only for a set amount of time, you reduce the likelihood that your thinking will turn to worry or that your quandary will affect the task at hand. Use **Thinking Aid 20** to remind you of this strategy when you begin to worry.

Stage II: Ante Up instead of Getting Out Or Giving In

The second strategy that builds insight might be described as "clinging to the mast during the storm." This tactic enables you to break away and maintain high spirits without lowering your goal when the problem is at its worst. Doing this requires *anteing up*: persisting when the problem is at its most difficult by adding

THINKING AID 20

BRACKETING TO MAINTAIN PERSPECTIVE AND POWER THINKING TOWARD PRODUCTIVE GAINS

- Set aside a designated time to consider options.

additional positive goals to your solution. **Thinking Aid 21** (on the facing page) will help remind you of this strategy.

Example: A friend of ours had recently married a man in his late 40's who had always been a loner. After the first year of marriage, it became apparent that her husband had developed the habit of calling her the moment any difficulty arose at his office. Our friend worked full time as well and felt that these frequent interruptions were unjust to her employer. We had taught her the **power thinking** strategy of *anteing up*, and she realized that she could use it to alleviate this problem. That evening, she explained to her husband the pluses and minuses of his behavior, and then offered an *ante up*. She explained that being allies in difficulties was a bond they had well established. They could now deepen their relationship by creating new methods of having *pleasurable, problem-free* bonds.

Specifically, she proposed that they make a pact to not discuss troubles that arose during the day until they both arrived home in the evening. At that time, they would have the choice of either solving the problem together, *or* — if the difficulty had already been solved by either party alone — they could discuss something else instead, or merely relax together. Soon her husband began looking forward to solving his own difficulties so that he could enjoy peaceful moments with his wife at home. Our friend solved her problem by finding an alternative that produced rewards beyond merely eliminating the problem — *anteing up*.

You can also *ante up* with yourself. When a problem escalates or your spirits drop, insight tends to offer only two solutions. You are tempted either to *get out* by disconnecting or running away; or to *give in* — sacrificing and compromising as much as possible so that the adversity will stop and you can at least salvage some of your original intent. When you feel you want to "get out" or "give

THINKING AID 21: ANTE UP INSTEAD OF GETTING OUT OR GIVING IN

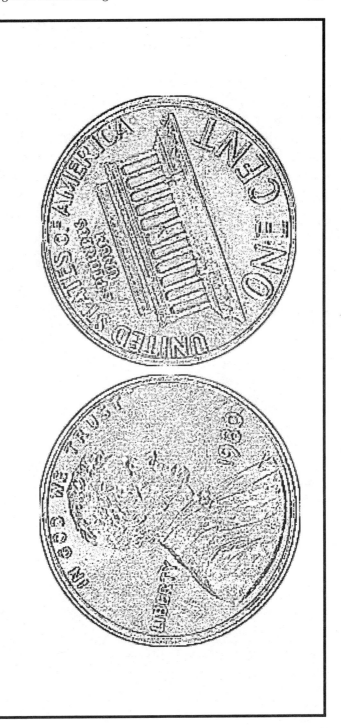

in," remind yourself that this is a signal that a new path of positive actions are about to be discovered if you will just "cling to the mast" a little longer. Specifically, *ante up* by altering and adding a new dimension to your original intention. This way, you will accomplish something positive instead of merely getting out of a situation or starting over by disconnecting from the problem.

Another indicator that *anteing up* would be valuable is when you feel boxed into a corner: when it seems that regardless of the step you take, you will lose. In such situations, establish a higher goal to attain in the present circumstances.

Example: A successful dieter credits *anteing up* with his ability to maintain his ideal weight. Specifically, when dieting becomes hard, he incorporates a new objective (in addition to merely losing weight) into his dieting goal, such as finding new, healthier foods and activities he enjoys that can be used for the rest of his life without gaining weight. Thus, dieting became the path to a healthy change of lifestyle.

Stage III: Vision Vs. Daydreams

Power thinkers visualize successful solutions before taking action. Less effective thinkers visualize failure scenarios — a tactic which undermines their performances. A powerful thinking strategy can trigger positive visions about problematic situations. We encourage you to say, "If we lived in a perfect world, what would I do? If I could create the perfect outcome, what would I do?"

Having a positive vision for the outcome will decrease the number of daydreams you pursue. The difference between visions and daydreams is that the latter are your illusions of receiving a desired goal *without personal effort*. Work and mental monitoring are inseparable from problem-solving success!

To distinguish the difference between visionaries and daydreamers, observe what you (and others) talk about. *Visionaries* describe actions they are taking to reach goals. *Daydreamers* talk about what others should do to reach a goal they desire, or they describe why "things haven't happened yet." **Thinking Aid 22** (on page 151) is

THINKING AID 22
VISION VS. DAYDREAMS

Daydream
VISION!

- I'm not daydreaming and expecting someone else to do the work for me.

- I have a vision and will do _____ to reach my goal.

designed to remind you of this **power thinking** strategy.

In summary: The three strategies that energize insight for problem-solving are *bracketing, anteing up,* and becoming a *visionary.*

SELF-KNOWLEDGE DURING PROBLEM SOLVING
Stage I: Build A Special Support Group

While you are already aware that support groups are important in life, power thinkers have special support groups. Members of their support groups believe in them unconditionally and display their support. In this group's eyes, they can never fail, even if some of their solutions do not produce the intended results. Further, this group satisfies the power thinkers' basic needs for survival, safety, acceptance, and self-esteem, and balances their weaknesses. When power thinkers "fail" to solve a problem, the support group motivates them to move on.

To establish such a support group, select others who are striving for the same goals as you are and who have similar personalities. Some will enjoy your personality and the relationship of past memories you share but do not independently pursue new challenges or goals. Some act as mentors, leading you to higher levels of success. Others will provide you with alternative points of view. Still others will provide resources, fun, and appreciation to celebrate your successes.

✍️ To determine if you have a strong support group, refer to the following list. In it, we have described characteristics that should be present in your group. Beside each quality, write the name(s) of people that supply that attribute for you. In the process, you will probably come to one quality for which you, yourself, are your own best support. As a matter of fact, if someone else attempts to offer that quality to you, you may become annoyed. Also, do not be concerned if the same person(s) is listed several times. Many people have such significant individuals in their lives who function effectively in several support roles. Now, we ask you to pause in your reading and list below the people in your support group who do each of these things for you.

Survival: _____

Counselor/Mentor: _____

Safety and Security: _____

Thorough and Accurate Follow-Through: _____

Acceptance: _____

Love: _____

Soulmate: _____

Self-Esteem, Ego Needs (*Gives you
compliments you remember and value*): _____

Appreciation: _____

Stimulates New Professional/Personal
Growth, Promotes Your Ideas: _____

Fun and Escape: _____

Work Toward New Goals: _____

Analyzing and Determining Reasons: _____

Opposes You but Commands Your Respect: _____

Up-to-Date and In Tune With Important Matters: _____

If any of the above are blank, seek people who possess that quality to add to your support group, and your problem-solving abilities will multiply.

Stage II: Overcoming Ineffective Beliefs About Success And Failure

Earlier in this chapter, you analyzed your beliefs about success and failure with **Thinking Tool H** (pp. 117-120). You removed unintentional, self-imposed barriers which inhibited your success in problem-solving. In particular, you may have held success as an

ideal so that you were unprepared to handle the increased responsibility it stimulates. Alternatively, you may have been so para-
lyzed by a fear of failure that you took few initiatives and did not
realize your full potential.

On the other hand, if you believe that you are in control of
your level of success, then you value a concept that correlates with
success and is common to people who have accomplished important goals in our society. If you perceive tasks to be malleable and
correctable, your self-resilience increases. Similarly, because you
believe you are in control of your problem, you will have a more
positive attitude about the possibility for success. Your success
rate will rise because of the confidence (self-respect) such an attitude generates.

To complete your self-analysis of beliefs about success and
failure, respond to the following questions.

🖎 Recall an event or project that did not end as successfully as
   you desired. Describe the reasons why that experience failed
   in your opinion:

   _____

   _____

🖎 What could *you* have done differently in order to reach greater
   success?

   _____

   _____

🖎 Now rephrase these reflections into something that you want
   to learn from this chapter to avoid future disappointments:

   _____

   _____

Stage III: Building Self-Efficacy And
Resilience Through Perseverance

Self-efficacy is defined as your assessment of your own ability to
overcome challenges. As you might suspect, problem solving is an

incremental skill. Power thinkers regard errors as natural, instructive parts of the problem-solving process. Because of this perspective, the need to have a successful solution for every task weighs less heavily upon their estimates of self-worth. If you develop this perspective, your *resilience* — your ability to "bounce back" from failure — expands. This resilience, in turn, elevates your problem-solving success by enabling you to override the repeated, early failures that often exist when problem solving begins.

On the other hand, if you do not accept an incremental skills perspective, you may see the number of successes you attain as a direct reflection of your general intellectual capability. As a result, you may steadily reduce the difficulty of tasks you select because such tasks present fewer chances for errors, are less threatening to your self-esteem, and permit you to easily display your intellectual proficiency. Unfortunately, *these tasks are also less likely to attain the success you desire.*

Power thinkers judge their success through consequence testing, not by imposing their own or society's criteria as the standard of effectiveness. They also allocate additional effort and ingenuity to the more difficult aspects of the task. They know which factors cannot be known and predict which method "feels" as if it will be effective (intuitive knowledge). However, if that method doesn't perform, they switch. This way, they examine multiple combinations of consequences. Moreover, power thinkers know that no amount of good luck, momentum, and enthusiasm can compensate when you do not do your homework. Thus, *perseverance* — continuing when the solution is not immediately apparent — is important.

Self-efficacy and resilience depend largely on having a realistic picture of what needs to be done and pacing yourself accordingly. The dividing line between extraordinarily successful people and less successful people is often a very small difference in performance, multiplied by perseverance.

Example: Vince Lombardi said that what distinguishes the truly great running back from a good running back is that the former runs five yards per carry. The latter runs four yards per carry. This one yard of difference comes from the extra effort that truly extraordinary running backs put forth, not from their clearly superior talent endowments.

✍ Think of the last time you experienced a setback. What did you do?

_____

_____

_____

_____

_____

Even the most successful quarterbacks may get sacked on one play, but they go on to throw a long pass for a touchdown on the next! If you develop your resiliency, you can *respond* to future failures instead of being defeated by them.

The ability to persevere often begins as an emotional connection to something, similar to falling in love. For it is the love of the project, your deep passionate care, that sustains **power thinking**. As Thomas Edison once said, "My genius is sticking to it!" When power thinkers are thrown into perplexities, they feel a burning desire to succeed.

Moreover, have you also noticed that when you persevere you learn more about your own virtues? Persistence develops patience toward yourself and others. One method of developing patience with tasks and other people is to develop the tenacity to perfect what you do yourself. When you work with such intensity to remove what the Bible refers to as the "boulders in your eyes," the "specks in others' eyes" are not as noticeable.

Last, you will know you have identified the correct problem when your problem statement begins with the word "I," not with "They," "He," or "She." Such statements place others in control of your problem.

Example: Suppose that you are annoyed because you have been in the doctor's waiting room for an exceedingly long period and there are still several people to be seen before you. You say to yourself: "Doctors are inconsiderate, conceited, and overpaid."

From this statement, you know you have not identified the challenge before you, because the word "I" does not appear in the statement you make. "I" must appear because the person facing a difficulty is *you*, not the doctor! For example, you could restate this difficulty by saying: "I am upset that I did not bring something to do while I wait. Since I know I have at least 15 more minutes before I see the doctor, what can I do now that will benefit me by saving me time later?"

Whenever you reword similar statements concerning difficulties, you have begun the *P*robing-*S*trategies-*P*roactively problem-solving process and are well on your way to rectifying the difficulty.

TO REVIEW

On the next page, let's reflect upon how you have grown from learning the strategies in this chapter, and how you will use them to address problems in the future.

✍ To review, rewrite the three stages in reasoning, insight, and self-knowledge that increase your problem-solving ability. Look back in the text to help yourself remember.

REASONING: 1. _____
(pages 123-145)
                    2. _____

                    3. _____

INSIGHT: 4. _____
(pages 145-152)
                    5. _____

                    6. _____

SELF-KNOWLEDGE: 7. _____
(pages 152-157)
                    8. _____

                    9. _____

✍ Last, recall the problem in which you wanted to become more successful that you described on page 116 at the beginning of this chapter. Write the strategy(ies) you want to use *now* to improve this situation.

_____

_____

✍ What is the most important change that has occurred in your thinking about this problem, as a result of reading this chapter?

_____

_____

_____

✍ If you write today's date here _____ , you can reread this chapter in the future and reflect upon how your thinking about problem solving has evolved.

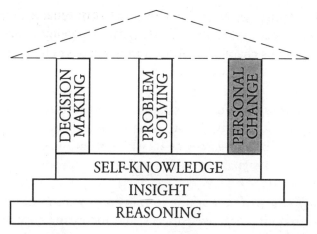

Reasoning:	Insight:	Self-Knowledge:
STOP: read/reflect/write	Break Away	Talents/Needs/Motives
ENTRAPMENT AND COST OF LOST OPPORTUNITY	*TELL BOTH SIDES TO CREATE RESOLUTION*	*CHANGE SELF, NOT OTHERS*
CAUTION: listen/ask questions	High Spirits	Analyze Beliefs
WHAT ABOUT THE PRESENT BRINGS PLEASURE?	*DEPRESSION*	*NEGATIVE PATTERNS*
GO: CAPped Speech	Create Flow	Strong Self-Concept
GO TO PERSON IN CHARGE	*PACE OF CHANGE*	*SELF-CREATIVITY*

CHAPTER 6
Power Thinking and Personal Change

Architects frequently demonstrate that a three-sided figure is the most stable. Similarly, the foundation for powerful thinking requires three elements: reasoning, insight, and self-knowledge; and success requires three areas of improvement: effective decision-making, proactive problem-solving, and productive personal change. In this chapter, we show how productive change incorporates all three foundation elements:

- *Reasoning:* identifying entrapments, opportunity costs, and the pleasure derived from present conditions;
- *Insight:* breaking away to act with resolution; using depression as a signal that changing at an appropriate pace is necessary;
- *Self-knowledge:* working to transform *yourself*, not others; overcoming negative patterns; and increasing creativity.

We define *change* as a qualitative improvement — becoming distinctly better. While the goals we identified in the introductory chapter of this book can be achieved without major changes in your life, some will progress more rapidly when strategies in this chapter are used to target ineffective aspects of present situations. We encourage you to read this entire chapter in one sitting. In the process, you will identify changes to some areas of your life which will assist you to reach the goals in this book. Then, when you have completed the chapter, you can apply the strategies reflectively and proactively at your preferred pace.

All productive change includes taking certain possible *risks:*

1. walking into new worlds of ideas that threaten your present beliefs;
2. experiencing initial feelings of inferiority in the presence of those who have lived among those ideas longer;
3. suspending judgment until you can see through the fog that covers new terrain; and
4. moving from the security of old, though unproductive, conditions to the volatility involved in change.

However, productive change results in *growth*, with the following benefits:

1. To this point in the book, we have described strategies for advancing your success without essentially transforming yourself. But if you are currently "stuck" in the wrong place, no amount of **power thinking** will put you in the right place without fundamental change. No matter how obvious this may seem, the strategies in this chapter are necessary because, without them, continuing in the same place will seem easier than starting all over in a new place.

2. Change gives you a competitive advantage because you become more innovative and more assertive at solving problems. Hollywood legend Gregory Peck once said in a television interview, "If you don't take a chance now and then to grow, you stand still — and then you begin to slide backward." Pat Riley, a successful professional basketball coach, once stated, "When you cannot make up your mind which of two evenly balanced courses of action to take — choose the bolder."

3. Successful change raises your aspirations because you know you have exceeded the best that you could have envisioned prior to the change.

Types of Personal Change

There are four types of personal change that can occur simultaneously: *physical, professional, intellectual,* and *interpersonal.* Each kind of change entails certain specific elements of risk, as depicted in **Thinking Aid 23** on the next page. However, in productive change, the benefits far outweigh the dangers.

The benefits of productive *physical change* are:

- increased self-esteem,
- increased attention from others,
- increased physical stamina, which improves your energy and strength for new goals in other areas of your life,
- better health, cardiovascular strength, and muscle tone, and
- the pleasure of reaching new heights physically.

THINKING AID 23

FOUR TYPES OF CHANGE = FOUR TYPES OF RISK

PHYSICAL CHANGE
= RISKING increased attention
from others and more de-
mands to say "no" effectively

CAREER CHANGE
= RISKING failure, lower
status initially, and possible
decrease in income

INTELLECTUAL CHANGE
= RISKING challenges to your
prior belief system, leaving
"black & white" thinking
behind

INTERPERSONAL CHANGE
= RISKING vulnerability,
rejection, entrapment

The benefits of *professional* or *career changes* are:

- increased self-awareness,
- confidence that you can succeed in difficult situations,
- the freedom that increased income affords,
- expanded satisfaction, and
- widening horizons for talent development.

The benefits of *intellectual changes* include:

- increased motivation that arises from acquiring new ideas,
- improved poise from successful mastery of "alien territories," and
- a broadened ability to address larger challenges in the future.

Interpersonal growth — the most neglected of all changes — means taking a chance to honestly "open up" to another person. When you share your most cultivated principles, those with similar ideas can align with you. In the process, you may gain an unexpected benefit to your self-esteem: another person who brings out the best in you, who beholds those valuable qualities in you that elude others, and who expands your sense of your own capabilities merely by being near. As Virginia Woolf put it:

> *My habits that had seemed durable as stone went down like shadows at the touch of another mind, and left behind a naked sky with fresh stars twinkling in it.*

You may be avoiding change at this time for a variety of reasons, including:

- fear of rejection,
- fear that others will interfere with or impede your true goals,
- fear of ridicule of your high self-expectations, and/or
- fear that the cost of giving up your self to gain alliance with another is too high a price to pay.

However, without changes and growth interpersonally, your personality becomes less stable and your ability to disclose genuinely to others decreases.

To better appreciate the difference between *changing* in these areas and merely *adding* new knowledge, think of a peak performance in a physical or career-type experience in your past. If, at the end of that experience, you allowed "a new you" to emerge, you changed. This enabled you to approach subsequent tasks with an expanded perspective.

We want to assist you to successfully change in the future. To do so, we would like you to take a simple test to determine which strategies you have not yet mastered, limiting your capacity for personal and professional change. To complete this self-reflective test, place a check before any of the following items that describe thoughts you have had in the past. The parentheses after each statement reference the strategy which addresses the obstacle described in each statement. After you mark an item, note the names and page numbers that describe these strategies. Attention to these pages will be particularly valuable for your abilities to grow through productive change.

For added professional gain, reread the checklist a second time. In this reading, each time the word "I" appears in a statement, substitute the words "my company." In this way, you can determine if your personal actions are limiting your company's abilities to grow through productive change.

Complete the following checklist by checking any item that may have kept you from changing in the past.

_____ 1. People won't like me if I change (*Negative Patterns*, p. 177).

_____ 2. I will think less of myself if I change (*Creativity*, p. 180).

_____ 3. I will not produce the desired results if the change fails (*Entrapment*, p. 167).

_____ 4. I refrained from changing in the past because I did not produce as much as I wanted. I spent so much time on the change process that other dimensions of my life faltered (*Cost of Lost Opportunity*, p. 167; *Pace of Change*, p. 173; *Creativity*, p. 180).

___ 5. I may fail and that would depress me (*Depression*, p. 173).

___ 6. I change when I perceive it will be exciting and/or valuable for others (*Negative Patterns*, p. 177).

___ 7. If I fail in the attempt at growth, I should think more highly of myself for having tried instead of not trying at all — but I probably won't (*Cost of Lost Opportunity*, p. 167).

___ 8. While most things in the world can be improved, I tend to listen too much to those who constantly find fault with me, others, and situations. As a result, my ideas and goals seem to diminish (*Entrapment*, p. 167).

___ 9a. When I think of a significant change in the past, the reason I changed was:_____.

9b. The reason I would make a similar change in the future is: _____.

(If the answers to 9a and 9b are different, you likely used strategies to create successful growth from your change. Also, if your answers differed, you are likely engaging in challenge for positive, growth-producing reasons, and a negative pattern is not affecting your life in this area. If the answer to both questions are the same, a negative pattern may be affecting your life in this area. See *Negative Patterns*, p. 177.)

___ 10. In the past, the same problems reoccurred after I changed (*Creativity*, p. 180).

___ 11. In the past, I have been asked to grow too fast (*Pace of Change*, p. 173).

___ 12. In the past, I invested too much time in trying to change and the effort was wasted (*Pace of Change*, p. 173).

___ 13. I hover over others (*Cost of Lost Opportunity*, p. 167).

____ 14. Because I am over-controlled by someone else, I feel that exploration is a waste of time (*Pace of Change*, p. 177).

____ 15. By restricting choices, I limit my ability to follow where my curiosity and passion lead (*Creativity*, p. 180).

____ 16. In the past, I can't remember changing unless I had had enough and finally got fed up (*Depression*, p. 173).

____ 17. When a challenge arose in the past, my first strategy was to assist others to change and alter their actions (*Changing Self*, p. 175).

____ 18. If it were a perfect world, what I would want others to do, and/or give to me is:

_____

(Whatever you write here is probably limiting your ability to change and grow. We become prisoners when we want someone to do for us, or to make us do for ourselves, what we must choose to do for ourselves. See *Changing Self*, p. 175.)

Example: If you wrote "I want others to truly understand me," subconsciously you may refrain from implementing a new idea until someone else has agreed it is valuable. Rather than seeking understanding from others, strive to understand more about yourself. Through this increased self-knowledge, you will better understand the purpose(s) for your goals, and you will no longer postpone actions until others convince you that you are correct. As an unintended benefit, this understanding will make it easier for *others* to understand you.

____ 19. I have someone who hovers over me. I compensate for this restrictive presence by allowing urges for change to go underground and hide until the person who hovers is not around. (*Entrapment*, p. 167).

_____ 20. What is it about my life now that brings me pleasure?

_____

_____

(*Analysis of what brings pleasure from present*, p. 169).

_____ 21. When I sought to change in the past but failed, the
first person I went to was:_____
(*Go to Person in Charge First*, p. 171).

_____ 22. I believe it is not good to discuss new plans for changes
with others (*Go to Person in Charge*, p. 171).

_____ 23. It is important that I suffer before I change (*Depression*, p. 173).

_____ 24. I do not change because I do not know how to protect myself from losing something that I cannot replace
(*Analyze what brings pleasure from present*, p. 169).

REASONING DURING PERSONAL CHANGE

Stage I: Analyze Entrapment
and Costs of Opportunities

The inability to analyze entrapment and costs of opportunities is one of the greatest obstacles to growth. *Entrapment* occurs
when one is lured or maneuvered into an uncomfortable, hope-
less, or compromised position without realizing it. Similarly, the
cost of opportunity means the cost (or loss) for having accepted an
opportunity, and thus giving up the other opportunities which
are mutually incompatible with the one you choose. This cost
must be weighed against the benefits that could accrue from the
opportunity you chose.

To avoid personal and professional entrapment and minimize
the costs of lost and inadequately accepted opportunities, measure
the opportunity and responsibilities against your goals or
company's mission before accepting. Is this opportunity moving
you (or your company) closer to what you truly want, and is it

consistent with the direction in which you want to proceed? If it isn't, subsequent opportunities will emerge that match these goals better.

Example: If you say to yourself, "I'd better do this just because the opportunity may never come again," you may be paying too high a cost for a change that is unlikely to be productive, and you are saying *yes* for the wrong reason, which creates entrapment. On the other hand, if you say to yourself, "This is the opportunity I've been waiting for, and I don't want to let it slip away," accepting the opportunity may expand your own, or your company's, life goals.

You will know you are entrapped personally when an experience, responsibility, or opportunity reduces your self-esteem instead of generating ideas for anteing up. Another signal of entrapment is when you decide to continue in the path of a past decision even when you realize that the decision was incorrect. You may choose to stay in a particular situation because you have already invested so much money, time, and effort into it and you overvalue this initial investment. Also, you like to believe that you make good decisions. Therefore, rather than acknowledging that a decision was incorrect, and working to understand what you can do to alter your course of action to eliminate this and future ineffective judgments, you continue to feel trapped. In such situations, you need to use the *decision-making* strategies (the DOUBLE THINK checklist, the WEIGHTED CHARACTERISTICS TEST, conquering human nature, saying *yes* and *no* appropriately, awaiting good indicators, and PR) to "un-entrap" yourself.

Similarly, when things don't happen in their allotted time, you must weigh the cost of lost opportunities against the possibility of entrapment to determine whether you should grant more time. You know tasks or goals just need more time when your self-esteem (or company morale) remains committed to your goals as difficulties increase. If high spirits continue to decrease, ask yourself how much loss you will allow. When this level is reached, either *ante up* or cut your losses — get out of the situation — to avoid entrapment. To do so, set a high ceiling and floor for your comfort zone. Listen to the high spirits of your insight. Think of what you (or your company) stand to gain, what you want, and what you can't live without.

In addition, to reduce opportunity cost, either "keep your feet moving" when new conditions diminish the chances for loss, or spend more time planning a better approach to overcome the challenge.

Example: One of the major differences between successful and less successful running backs in football is that the former never stop moving their feet forward when a tackler grabs them; the less successful give up right away.

Therefore, you can avoid entrapment and the too-high costs of ill-accepted opportunities if you change by analyzing your goals, keeping your feet moving, and knowing when you will cut your losses or ante up in difficulties.

Stage II: Analyze What Brings Pleasure in Your Present Habits

The next obstacle to change is failure to analyze what it is about present situations that brings you pleasure (or brings your company new potential for growth). When we do not know the reasons why we like things the way they are, we subconsciously guard ourselves by resisting changes in *everything* about that situation. Because we do not know what is special in a situation, we try to maintain *all* aspects of it for fear of "throwing the wheat out with the chaff."

To complete this analysis, first think about an aspect of your life or company that you wish to change, and list *two positives and two negatives* about that aspect. Doing so ensures that you identify the initial good intent that the situation was established to perform, and how that intent is or is not being actualized.

✍ To practice, list two *positive* aspects of a condition that you
   want to change:

   _____

   _____

✍ Now list two *negative* aspects of that condition:

   _____

   _____

✍ Now, what can you change about the two negative items you
   listed above, either through physical, intellectual, interpersonal, or professional changes, that would contribute more
   to yourself and/or others?

   _____

   _____

Last, analyzing what brings you pleasure personally can include another important component. By increasing the number
of risks you take in *all four categories of productive change*, your personality becomes more well-rounded. Such simultaneous changes
"smooth your rough edges." Without such venturings, you will
experience more stress than other people because the foundation
for your self-esteem becomes less stable.

✍ To begin, return to the category of risks that are most difficult for you. Do so by listing the six productive changes you
   have accomplished in your life that most rapidly come to
   mind. Write them quickly below:

   1. _____

   2. _____

   3. _____

   4. _____

   5. _____

   6. _____

Reread this list. Are physical, intellectual, interpersonal, and career changes all present? If not, using the strategies in this chapter for growth *in the areas not represented* will bring the greatest and most immediate pleasure and gain for you personally. We encourage you to do so.

Stage III: Go to the Person in Charge First

To grow productively, *go to the person in charge* and ask questions that assist you to take the first step toward change and understand the five underlying causes of negative patterns that affect successful change in that area. To see if you presently take this step in reasoning about change, answer the following question.

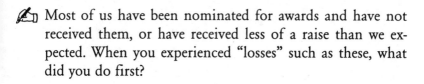 Most of us have been nominated for awards and have not received them, or have received less of a raise than we expected. When you experienced "losses" such as these, what did you do first?

_____

_____

Some people try to reason through the failure alone until they think of (what they consider to be) the most plausible explanation. Others go to the person in charge, but only to protest or demand an explanation, and to leave the image that they were mistreated or misunderstood.

The alternative, more successful change path, however, is to *seek advice* as to how you can improve in the area of your loss so that you increase your abilities. When you want to change, and especially when you have suffered a loss you want to reverse, go to a person in charge (or one who has succeeded in a similar change) *before* you develop your plan of action.

Example: One of our favorite examples occurred after the 1993 Orange Bowl. In that game, the University of Nebraska lost to Florida State because its passing defense was too weak. Three days later, Tom Osborne, the Nebraska head coach called Bobby Bowden, the head football coach at Florida State University, who had created the strongest passing defense in the country. Bobby Bowden agreed to send his assistant coaches for one week to assist the University of Nebraska coach. In 1995, the University of Nebraska won the national championship.

INSIGHT DURING PERSONAL CHANGE

Stage I: Create Resolution by Telling the Upsides and Downsides

Why are some people able to take the information in this book and turn their lives around, while others will change nothing? The answer is *action*. **Power thinking** enables you to create ways of searching for *new* concepts and move beyond merely altering things that are unsatisfactory in a present experience. We have all had someone tell us about a weakness we turned to strength:

Example: "You have a chip on your tooth, your Adam's apple sticks out too far, and you talk too slow. You can never be a movie star."

— a Universal Pictures Executive in a casting call review, to Clint Eastwood.

Change means turning limitations into strengths through the four types of change, analyzing whether entrapment exists, and going to the person in charge.

Example: Thomas Edison did not create the light bulb by thinking of ways to alter a candle. Instead, he searched for an entirely *new* concept to eliminate the limitations. With each unsuccessful effort, he refined his knowledge about the qualities that would be necessary for better, future illumination to occur.

When old ideas are eliminated, and new, better ones take their place, an uncomfortable or painful period of exploration and confusion may occur. This confusion will be eliminated when you act with resolution and help people — others as well as yourself — understand *why* you are changing. You can do so by *telling people both sides of every decision*, as illustrated in **Thinking Aid 24** on the next page. When people know the "upsides and downsides," they feel you are being honest with them, so they will commit more completely and can help make changes more positive. Intuitively, people know there will be some downsides to change, and if they do not start by analyzing the reasons for their resistance, they may react negatively on the basis of their nebulous fears. If you have proactively helped settle those fears by concretely identifying the potential downsides, you will be rewarded with their increased trust and support.

Stage II: Depression

Depression is the absence of high spirits. It serves as a warning that your conscious reasoning is not yet ready to recognize that the "old self" and "the way things used to be" are outdated. Depression can be a signal that major change is required for successful and evolutionary adaptation. In this sense, as described in Chapter 3, the subconscious is one step ahead of your conscious reasoning.

Thus, we encourage you to always use depression (emotional in your personal life, and economically in your professional life) *as a signal* that you or your company needs a physical (fiscal), intellectual (management), career (marketing), or interpersonal (personnel) change. When depression occurs, the problem solving and decision making strategies in Chapters 4 and 5 alone are not sufficient for the job. Depression means you need to stop trying to remedy the present situation and, instead, to bring completely new changes into the arena.

Stage III: Know Your Pace of Change

Knowing the pace at which you can respond most positively to change increases your confidence because you will allow your-

THINKING AID 24
TELL PEOPLE THE DOWNSIDES AND UPSIDES
TO POTENTIAL CHANGES

UPSIDES
- Certain benefits
- Potential benefits

DOWNSIDES
- Certain losses
- Possible losses (Risks)

self the necessary "wait time" so that your self-concept can rise to the challenge of the change. Compared to those around you, you may change slowly (and consider yourself to be conservative) or rapidly (and consider yourself to be an activist). If you judge yourself to be more conservative than others, you will permit yourself to bring more objects and features of past conditions with you into a newly changing situation so that your adjustment will be easier. If you change rapidly, ask yourself daily (as you pick up your purse or briefcase to leave at the end of each working day): "What did I do or change today that caused me and/or my company to grow?"

SELF-KNOWLEDGE DURING PERSONAL CHANGE
Stage I: Change Yourself First, Not Others

To become optimally successful, it is important to know that the first person who needs to alter his or her actions and thinking in difficult situations is you. When you face a challenge, if you look inside to grow to overcome the difficulties rather than expecting others to change, you will achieve more productive results. For example, when interacting with an annoying person, less successful people think about how to change that person — what will enable them to escape from the person or the problem. Successful people look inside themselves, however, to see why that interaction is annoying them and what they can do to stop the negative feelings they are experiencing.

Example: The president of a corporation had difficulty listening to Stanley, the company's comptroller. It was evident that Stanley needed to talk, but he did not know how to **CAP** his speech, and not many people would take the time to listen to him. However, the president used the strategy of changing himself first — improving his listening ability. As he did, Stanley began to share more innovative thoughts, which the president and Stanley put into action to assist others in the company to think more productively about financial matters.

The reason you must begin by changing yourself and not others is that changes in yourself reinforce changes in others. The changes you initiate in others are more prone to spontaneous recovery when they are not backed up by changes in you. *Spontaneous recovery* is the subconscious's inclination to revert to habitual ways, regardless of the conscious mind's desire to discard previous patterns. Also, when you begin by expecting others to change, you tend to:

- blame them for not meeting your (usually unexpressed) expectations,
- assume that they *purposely* avoided fulfilling your expectations, and
- misinterpret their neglect as a clear message that they no longer value the company or yourself as much as you do them.

In such situations, when an expectation is not returned, turn your question(s) to yourself — toward understanding your own needs. In other words, instead of trying to predict why someone did not meet your expectation, ask yourself why you assumed that that person *should* have met it. Whenever you hear yourself asking: "I wonder why So-and-so did not (or did) _____ ," turn your question inward: "Why did I want that person to do _____ for me? What can *I* do to fulfill what I expected?"

✍ Let's practice this strategy. Think of a person who recently did not do something that you wanted (or expected) him or her to do. Write that experience here:

_____

_____

✍ Write why you wanted (or expected) that person to do the above:

_____

_____

✍ What is it that you needed and did not receive in this situation?

_____

✍ Now, think of ways that *you* can fill the void you expected the other person to fill. List them here.

_____

_____

_____

Stage II: Overcoming Negative Patterns

A *negative pattern* occurs when an unidentified need guides your life to change in ways that are unproductive. Negative patterns are caused by five interacting forces:

1. lack of mastery of one or more **power thinking** strategies;
2. unidentified, unfulfilled needs;
3. limited experience in one or more of the four types of change processes described in this chapter;
4. failure to analyze surrounding circumstances and apply ADAPT creativity strategies (see pages 180-183); and
5. misconceptions.

Overcoming the negative patterns that influence your life helps your changes produce more sustained benefits, because you will neither generalize too much from single incidents nor classify recurring events as unrelated incidents. In the examples on the subsequent pages, we ask that you identify the five causes of the pattern that limited each person's growth through change. Then we ask you to identify patterns occurring in your life that are limiting your ability to grow through productive change. When you have addressed *all* the causes, the negative pattern will disappear.

Therefore, to identify negative patterns that limit growth in your life, identify the possible multiple causes by:

1. Using Chapter 10 (which lists all the **power thinking** strategies) to identify which strategies you have not yet mastered.
2. Applying reasoning, insight, and/or self-knowledge to identify a need that is overshadowing your **power thinking** in an area in which the negative pattern of repeated failure exists.
3. Identifying which of the four types of changes you have the least experience making, and how this inexperience may be affecting your life (or company).
4. Analyzing the circumstances that surround your negative pattern, and using ADAPT creativity strategies (pp. 180–183) to alter negative aspects of these circumstances.
5. Identifying a misconception that exists in this situation which guided past actions.

Before you apply this analysis to a personal or professional situation in your life, see if you can determine the five causes of the negative pattern that exists in the following situations.

Example 1:   Some husbands are not aware that they want to limit their wives' success. Such husbands may complain and become helpless when their wives are out of town on business. They may ask their wives to be home to cook dinner at a specified time. They may set limits on the amount of outside activities in which their wives can be involved. They may begin delegating more menial, home-based tasks to their wives, unconscious of their underlying intent of reducing her interests outside of the home.

✍ What negative pattern is occurring in the lives of such husbands and wives, in your opinion, and what strategy do you recommend that they use to overcome it?

_____

_____

_____

You may have written that the wife is beginning to dread telling her husband about out-of-home commitments and therefore waits till the last minute to tell him. As a result, the husband is increasingly nervous, as he waits to be shocked by the next evidence that his wife's career is growing rather than her becoming more subservient to his needs. The pattern developed because the husband did not reason to identify why he wanted his wife to alter her career. The strategies the husband and wife should use are:

- the *Reasoning* strategies discussed in Chapter 2, and
- *asking questions* to identify what priorities are important to him and to her, so that both of them can recognize the stimulus for his patterned behavior.

Without these strategies, such husbands and wives may remain unable to recognize the ramifications of their negative pattern of relating to each other.

Example 2: Similarly, some wives want to control their husbands. They point out negative events outside, or inside, the home that make them unhappy. These actions are an attempt to maintain their husbands' total focus. For example, one woman may talk negatively about others and blame her problems on others' or her husband's conditions and actions, rather than her own behaviors. She becomes highly skilled at convincing everyone that what she does is for her husband's best interest — when in reality she is manipulating and dominating him so he will become subservient to, and under the command of, her whims. In this way, *she* does not have to change.

✍ What is the stimulus for this negative pattern?

_____

_____

Now, turn your attention inward.

✍ Identify something you have tried to change in the past but
   have repeatedly failed to accomplish.

_____

✍ What are the five causes for your repeated pattern of failure?

1. _____
2. _____
3. _____
4. _____
5. _____

✍ What can you do to eliminate these causes?

_____

_____

_____

_____

_____

Stage III: Creativity

Creativity is the ability to bring into existence or make out of
nothing something for the first time; or, to bring about a new
course of action or behavior. It is also one of the most valuable
tools for change. Economists predict that half of today's students
will depend upon their creative thinking abilities for livelihoods
in the 21st century, and that within 10 years, most promotions
and career options will be based on a person's ability to generate
new ideas and approaches to problems rapidly. Also, physicians
have proven that creativity and some of its by-products, such as
humor and laughter, have positive effects on circulation, respira-
tion, pain thresholds, immunity, pulse rate, endorphins, and oxygen levels in the blood. Creativity also breaks down resistance and
builds unity in group settings.

Unfortunately, for most of us, creativity has to be developed. Five strategies increase creativity, and we use the acronym **ADAPT** to remember them, as illustrated in **Thinking Aid 25** (on the next page).

*A*dapt = Change a small detail in a first idea. To do so, look for a stronger detail or a more specific way to communicate a new image. This search (*A*dapt) will build your creativity and keep you from having to begin anew.

Decrease = Change by eliminating or compressing ideas. Reduce time, space, and elaborations by connecting only salient features to make effective changes. For example, a feeling of confusion is often your insight's call to "decrease." Some advertisers use the *D*ecrease strategy by reducing their television commercials from 30 to 15 seconds to increase the creativity of the commercials, which leads to increased sales. For another example, think of your most respected colleague. Is this person the one who speaks the *most* at meetings — or the one who *succinctly* states a new, effective idea?

*A*dd = Add parts by asking "What else is possible?" For example, professional cartoonists have discovered that drawings take on new, innovative personalities when the cartoonist simply adds pressure to his strokes, making bolder outlines on the figures, rather than through hours of contemplation trying to make the features of the face or body unique.

Position differently = Change by reprioritizing details, or placing ideas in different relationships to one another. Such repositioning involves brainstorming so that you can create unlikely combinations. For example, the persons who designed the car telephone, the reclining chair, and portable-headset stereos used this strategy to combine unlike objects, uniting the best features of each into a single concept. The probable originality of your outcome increases when you link the key elements of twenty ideas together rather than when you produce only two.

THINKING AID 25
"ADAPT" CREATIVELY TO CHANGE MORE EFFECTIVELY

 dapt your first idea by changing only one detail

 ecrease or compress one section of your idea

 dd parts by asking what else is possible

 osition differently by reprioritizing details

ake charge and change parts under your control

*T*ake charge = Change by altering parts under your control when anguish begins. By using the *T*ake Charge strategy while you await illumination, you will be less likely to ascribe your frustrations to personal inadequacy. The most positive feature of *T*aking Charge will be the fostering of a greater willingness to persist in trying to solve a challenging situation, in spite of the frustrations you may feel.

Now, let's discuss ADAPT in action through a real example. In the following illustration, creative change and ADAPT strategies become a part of one person's **power thinking** repertoire at an early age, thanks to his parents.

Example: A mother in the 1950s fostered creativity in her son at a young age. The son, a Boy Scout, wanted to earn a merit badge in filmmaking. His father had bought him a Super-8 movie camera. The child had the inspiration to make a horror movie. For one shot, he needed red, bloody-looking gook to ooze from kitchen cabinets. So his mother went out, bought thirty cans of cherries, and cooked them in a pressure cooker, creating a delightfully oozy red gook (*D*ecrease in size). The gooey bloody kitchen scene, she recalled much later, left her picking cherries out of cupboards for years!

Then, she gave her son free rein of the house (*T*ake charge), letting him convert it into his film studio (*A*dapt or change details), moving furniture around (*P*osition differently), putting backdrops over things (*A*dd to make a change). She helped him make costumes and even acted in his films. When he wanted a desert scene, she drove him out to the desert in their Jeep (*P*osition differently), etc., etc.

This son's name is *Steven Spielberg*.

✍ To review and reinforce what you have learned about your personal and professional abilities to grow through productive change, list all the strategies you can recall. For any strategy you cannot recall, return and skim the information on the pages we list below so that you can use the strategy to overcome limitations in your ability to change productively in the future.

REASONING: 1. _____
(pages 167-172)
                  2. _____

                  3. _____

INSIGHT: 4. _____
(pages 172-175)
                  5. _____

                  6. _____

SELF-KNOWLEDGE: 7. _____
(pages 175-183)
                  8. _____

                  9. _____

To conclude: In what "new world" have you been called to invest your expertise? Each time you change successfully you will leave the known, and walk into a cool, damp fog surrounding the unfamiliar which extends ahead, beyond the limits of your present capabilities. As you expand your expertise, this fog will part before you, enabling others to more easily follow in your footsteps. At the same time, you will change. Subsequently, when you turn around to view the familiar terrain that lies in the distance behind, it will no longer require the growth you so recently labored to establish; that growth will already have become part of you. With **power thinking**, a new best will await you ahead in the fog. Unfortunately, without successful change and **power thinking**, the familiar terrain of your past will be all that you have in your present and future.

CHAPTER 7
Work-Related Applications

If we reflect upon our lives, we can all think of bad decisions we have reached. We have purchased stocks that lost money. We have been offered jobs and known from day one that taking the job was a mistake. We can also think of the "roads not taken" in our career paths.

Just as we can think of bad decisions we have made, we can also think of good ones: for example, recommendations we were asked to make that ultimately proved successful.

We can also look at business corporations where both good and bad decisions have occurred. Lee Iacocca described the problems at Chrysler in his autobiography *Iacocca*. We've seen airlines that went bankrupt. The Edsel is obsolete. Conversely, we have seen bold decisions that have resulted in tremendous successes. Examples are the birth of personal computers, VCRs, microwaves, Henry Ford's decisions with the Model T, and George Washington's military successes in the Revolutionary War.

As you recall decisions you have made, actions you took or did not take, and as you think about the current decisions you are pondering now, you may believe you reached your decisions purely on luck. Conversely, you may have used specific strategies that helped you reach your success.

In Chapters 7, 8, and 9, we want to show you how we apply **power thinking** to everyday problems, using examples from professional, personal, and family situations. We begin with three work-related situations in which you can practice applying **power**

thinking in real-world settings. For two problems, we first present the situation. Then we set out the course of our thinking as we apply the **power thinking** strategies we have been describing. These will illustrate how we thought through the problem situation to arrive at a decision for action. If you desire, you can work through your course of thinking and compare the strategies you would have used in each situation to our thinking course. The third situation is presented for you to work out yourself. If you are interested in how we addressed the issues in this third situation, look at the Appendix at the end of this chapter.

SITUATION 1 (DECISION-MAKING): STAN

Stan, age 36, has recently moved to a new city. He has begun to play golf. Although he is a very good athlete in general, due to his newness to golf, he is not a very good golfer. Recently, Stan's boss invited Stan to play in his golf league. On the one hand, Stan sees this as an excellent opportunity to meet many new people in the city who would be assets to his business and an opportunity to get to know his boss better. Playing in the league would also be an impetus to practice playing golf and to improve his game more rapidly.

On the negative side, Stan is really a poor golfer. He is a firm believer that you never get a second chance to make a first impression. He is concerned that people will make a decision on his professional competence based on his golf ability. Since Stan is new on the job, he is also concerned about taking the time to play golf one day a week. The day of the league is on the busiest day of the week for him, as his weekly report is due which normally takes eight hours to complete to the level of quality he desires.

Stan must let his boss know by this afternoon what his decision is. He calls you and asks to meet with you to discuss the matter. When he comes to your office, he tells you has also discussed it with another friend, Donna. He and Donna employed four **power thinking** strategies, and it was her advice that he should play in the league.

What thinking processes would you use with Stan in order to make a decision? (We realize that some of your strategies may be the same as those Donna used with Stan, and some will be different, based on your own personality.)

_____

_____

_____

_____

_____

_____

_____

_____

_____

_____

_____

_____

_____

_____

_____

At the end of your meeting, Stan asks you for a "bottom line." What do you recommend?

_____

If you are wondering what Stan really did do, here's how he reached his decision. First, he referred to the summary of decision-making strategies at the beginning of Chapter 4. This was his thought process, including the strategies he used to make his decision:

1. He knew he did *not* need to "do a DOUBLE-THINK" with the **DOUBLE THINK Checklist (Thinking Tool D,** p. 75), since this decision did not involve anyone other than himself.

2. He read the **Excuses List (Thinking Tool F,** p. 87) and realized that he was using Excuses 16 ("I don't have time") and 17 ("I don't because it makes me feel uncomfortable"), so he wrote the following:

   • "I control my time, so I'll rearrange my schedule and write my report one day early each week," and

   • "I'll overcome my discomfort by preparing a creative, humorous statement to introduce myself to league members so as to make a good impression and overcome the possibility that they will judge my professional competence based on my golf ability alone."

3. The second strategy Stan used was the **Weighted Characteristics Test (Thinking Tool E,** p. 83). We have inserted a copy of his completed scale in **Figure 7-1** on the next page.

4. The third strategy Stan used was to **complete a personal assessment** to see the level of self-respect he would feel if he played golf. When he did this, he realized that he would really be sure it was the right decision if he could **"ante up"** (p. 146). This would mean *adding his talents to the decision.* He would set and accomplish several specific goals for business, pleasure, exercise, stress reduction, and personal/professional growth each week. Since Stan is an excellent "goal setter" and "accomplisher," playing golf could become profitable for him in many aspects of his life.

5. Last, Stan **broke away** from his reasoning and personal analysis to allow his insight to have some input. He knew that if he felt good indicators by that afternoon when his boss called for his decision, playing golf would be the best decision. He felt these good indicators almost immediately.

Therefore, Stan joined the league, and it was the correct decision for him.

FIGURE 7-1
STAN'S WEIGHTED CHARACTERISTICS TEST (COMPLETED)

PLAY GOLF		DO NOT PLAY GOLF	
1. Meet new clients	9	1. Could be made fun of because I'm a poor golfer	1
2. Know my boss better	8	2. Could make bad first impression	7
3. Practice golf to improve my game	2	3. Could take too much time from work	6
4. Get exercise	4	4. Playing will require that I find a way to do my report early	5
5. Reduce stress	3		
TOTAL	**26**	**TOTAL**	**19**

SITUATION 2 (PROBLEM SOLVING): WALLACE

Wallace is the chief executive officer of a relatively large and successful company. Wallace's company has three locations, all within the United States. At the last meeting with the board of directors, several of them again urged him to examine the feasibility of opening one or two plants in foreign countries. Wallace voiced philosophical arguments against doing so. He indicated that he strongly believed that his consumers were Americans and that, since his company was profiting from American customers, American workers should be the beneficiaries of the profits. He also believed that the quality of the goods would decrease if produced in a foreign country.

His board members argued that overseas manufacturing would produce greater profits, which could be used to pay larger salaries to American workers as well as to assure the long-range welfare of the company. They also said that there were numerous examples of quality products made outside of North America.

You are a vice-president in that company, and Wallace asks

you to help him resolve this difficulty. Luckily, you have at your fingertips the **power thinking** strategies for problem solving in Chapter 5.

✎ Describe the thinking processes you will utilize with Wallace in order to reach the decision to be presented at the next board meeting.

_____

_____

_____

_____

_____

_____

_____

_____

_____

_____

_____

_____

_____

_____

✎ Based on the information presented, what solution do you think you would reach?

_____

_____

_____

This was Wallace's actual thought process and strategy selection.

1. Wallace realized that the problem involved a conflict of beliefs (his own beliefs against those of the Board of Directors). Therefore, he **evaluated his beliefs**, using **Thinking Aid 6** on page 57, to make sure that his own beliefs were constructive and valid.

2. He also completed **Thinking Tool I** (p. 124): **Solving Problems Involving Other People by Probing for the Best Interactive Pattern**. As a result, he decided to retain his personal position.

3. However, he still needed to convince the Board of Directors that his decision was the best one. To do this, he prepared **matrices** (pp. 126-132) to show the likely interactions of three possible situations: two foreign plants, two American plants, or one foreign and one American plant.

4. When he presented all three matrices to the Board of Directors, he closed by **telling both the upsides and downsides** of his plan. Objectively presenting three alternatives helped the Board discern the facts more clearly and support Wallace's decision not to open any plants overseas.

SITUATION 3 (PERSONAL CHANGE): LUCINDA

Lucinda is a 43-year-old single mother of two children, ages 16 and 11. She has been a teller for seven years at a bank that has multiple branches throughout the city and region. Lucinda was recently summoned to the bank headquarters and presented with the possibility of assuming a new job: the position of Assistant Bank Manager. The primary duties of the position would be community relations. The community relations activities would require several evening and weekend functions, as well as personnel evaluations in which Lucinda would primarily work with bank employees experiencing difficulties. It was also conveyed that if she were to take this position, it would mean a large salary increase, and if she performed satisfactorily within five years, new opportunities for advancement would occur.

This job offer presented a real dilemma for Lucinda. As a single mother, she could really use the money for immediate as well as long-term needs. It would also mean doing one function — working with colleagues — that she really wanted to do.

On the downside (for her), it was made clear to her that her direct contact with customers would be virtually non-existent. She regarded many of her present customers as friends and truly relished interacting with them when they came to the bank. She was also concerned about the evening and weekend responsibilities of the job. Her children were at an age when they needed a lot of parental support. Since her ex-husband was out of state, the burden of parenting fell solely and directly upon her.

After receiving this opportunity for professional change, Lucinda has lunch with you. As a friend, she tells you about the offer. She asks for your advice as to whether she should take this job or not. The two of you work through the decision together by using her responses to strategies from this book.

In the space below, think through your approach to this situation, referring to Chapter 6 (Personal Change) to help you. Write out your decision process in as much detail as you can. Then make the final decision. See page 194 for our recommendations.

✍ What strategies would you select and why?

_____

_____

_____

_____

_____

_____

_____

_____

_____

_____

_____

_____

_____

_____

_____

_____

_____

_____

_____

✍ What would be the ultimate decision?

_____

The process of professional decision making will not always be this time-consuming. We would now like you to think of a difficult professional challenge you have had to make in the past. On a separate sheet of paper, write down:

1. the issue that you faced, describing its various elements;
2. the strategies, if any, you used to reach the decision; and
3. the decision you ultimately made.

Since you have learned several new strategies by reading this book, what strategies would you use now? Would the resulting decision be the same or different?

Now think of a professional decision that either you, a friend, or a member of your family is currently facing. What strategies would you suggest to this person?

Professional decisions are not the only ones we have to reach. There are also decisions we have to make personally, and in family relations. In the next two chapters, we will present examples of personal and family relations. We will use the same model to help you practice applying **power thinking** to your decision-making process.

APPENDIX: LUCINDA

These are the strategies we suggested:

1. First, in offering advice, we would ask **questions**.
2. Help her analyze which choice brings **good indicators**.
3. Analyze **entrapment versus cost of lost opportunities**.
4. Analyze **what about present situation — and possible new job — would bring pleasure**.
5. **Go to the person in charge** — two people who took a similar job or did not take a similar job — to seek advice before she makes her decision.
6. Analyze the **pace of change** from which she has profited in the past.
7. Analyze if there is any **ADAPT** way to have the best of both worlds.
8. Use the **DOUBLE THINK Checklist**.
9. Use the **Weighted Characteristics Test** to end the session.

CHAPTER 8
Personal Life Applications

In Chapter 7, we demonstrated the application of **power thinking** techniques to real-life professional situations. In the same manner, we now present three examples of challenges you might encounter in your personal life. For the first two situations, we present the scenario, then set out the course of our thinking as we applied the **power thinking** strategies we have been describing. These examples will illustrate how we thought through the problem situation to arrive at a decision for action. If you desire, you can work through your own course of thinking and compare the strategies you used in each situation to our thinking course. The third situation is presented for you to work out yourself. Our suggestions appear at the end of the chapter.

SITUATION 1 (DECISION-MAKING): GLEN

Four years ago, Glen was asked by a group of people to run for the school board. There were three openings and five people ran. Glen finished fifth and was a large margin from being in the top three. It is now four years later, and a group of people have come to ask Glen to run for school board again. He wants to do it, but he was humiliated by losing by such a large margin in the last race. What thinking processes should Glen use to make this decision?

Let us suppose that you are a friend of Glen's, and that he has come to you for advice before making his decision. What advice would you give him? Stop reading this book until you have thought of your strategy process and written it below. The summary of **power thinking** strategies for decision making presented at the beginning of Chapter 4 will help you.

✍ Describe the thinking processes you will utilize with Glen.

_____

_____

_____

_____

_____

_____

_____

_____

_____

_____

_____

_____

_____

_____

_____

_____

_____

_____

_____

✍ Based on the information presented, what solution do you think you and Glen would reach?

_____

_____

Here is how Glen actually reached his decision. He referred to the summary of decision-making strategies from Chapter 5. This was his thought process, including the strategies he used to make his decision.

1. During the **STOP stage of reasoning,** he called the three people who won the election last time. They described their successful campaigns and told Glen which parts of the campaign they considered to be most successful. This preliminary research told Glen what steps he could take to improve his chances if he did decide to run.

2. During the **CAUTION stage of reasoning,** he found six people who had not voted for him in the last election. He asked them to state the reasons they had not supported him, and also what they wanted a new board member to do. From these people, Glen learned that he had not appeared passionate enough about the issues and had not posed difficult questions to his opponents.

3. During the **GO stage of his reasoning,** Glen made a list of all the excuses he had given himself and others as to why he had lost before, and all the excuses he was tempted to use for not running again. Then he **wrote statements he could use to replace his excuses,** in **Figure 8-1** (on the next page).

4. Next, Glen **analyzed his beliefs** about his freedom to say *yes* or *no*. However, he realized that he did not have any difficulty saying either *yes* or *no* to this group, so that was not a factor exerting negative influence upon his decision.

5. Last, Glen **analyzed how strong his self-concept would be** if he said *yes* or *no*. If he said *yes*, was he being truthful to himself and his constituency? Could he honestly, naturally, and passionately project the image and person they desired to fill this level of responsibility? Would he be saying *yes* just for the glory? Alternatively, if he said *no*, would he regret that he had not at least tried? Could he commit to the responsibility of being the best school board member possible and still maintain the level of responsibility and success he wanted in his job?

FIGURE 8-1

EXCUSE I CAN'T/SHOULDN'T BECAUSE...	POWERFUL REPLACEMENT I CAN AND WILL BECAUSE...
1. I ran last time and lost. I am afraid of losing again and being humiliated by my failure.	1. If I follow the advice I received from my colleagues, I am less likely to fail this time.
2. I'm not sure I can do a good job if I win.	2. "The job maketh the man" (a quotation I learned once).
3. I don't think I have the personality to be a Board member.	3. My friends are encouraging me to run, so they must think I do — or else they want me to run for other reasons that are more important than the match of my natural personality to the job.

6a. To answer these questions with self-knowledge, insight, and reasoning, Glen set aside time to **await good indicators** from his insight. He did this by **breaking away** each evening of the week before the filing deadline in order to answer the questions he posed for himself above, to plan actions he could take during his campaign, and to think of propositions he would suggest if he got on the board.

6b. During these break-away periods, he also thought of the person he admired most — his father — and envisioned how his father would make this decision. In doing so, he recalled that the qualities he admired most in his father were his humility and his genius for identifying and promoting just the right person for the job. As he reflected, Glen recalled how good he felt when he himself exercised those talents, and how often people told him he, too, was gifted in these areas.

6c. Suddenly, Glen was struck with an insight. He recalled how rapidly his friend Jeff had risen in popularity from his work on the United Way campaign this year. He recalled how adamantly Jeff had talked about changes that were needed in the schools, and how Jeff's ideas were applauded at the PTO meeting last month. What a fantastic board member *Jeff* would make! In fact, Glen thought, Jeff would really be the ideal board member.

If Glen became Jeff's campaign manager, he could lend his management, organizational, and promotional skills to the school board without trying to become something he wasn't. And if he and Jeff acted on all the knowledge Glen had gained in the process of making this decision, Jeff would probably win the election! Glen's **good indicators** had arrived — he was delighted with this decision.

Glen called Jeff immediately. After many hours of dedicated work by both of them, Jeff won a position on the school board, where he helped implement many effective innovations. Glen was pleased and satisfied with his decision.

SITUATION 2 (PROBLEM SOLVING): JAN

Your friend Jan fears public speaking, but at her son's request, she agreed to speak to his ninth-grade class about the benefits and sacrifices of her career choice. The following week, the high school principal called Jan and asked her to be one of five parents to serve on a panel for the school's annual presentation to the student body concerning career choices. Jan would like to do it but is afraid of embarrassing herself or her son — or her workplace, as several of her own employees will be in the audience.

The principal suggests that Jan take a day to think about it. You have now devoted several hours to thinking about our ideas in this book. Let's suppose that Jan asks you for advice.

What strategies do you suggest to Jan?

_____

_____

_____

_____

_____

_____

_____

_____

_____

_____

_____

_____

_____

_____

_____

_____

_____

_____

_____

Based on the information presented, what solution do you think you would reach together?

_____

_____

_____

Below are the strategies we suggested to Jan and the results of her Problem-Solving Process. How does your list compare to our list?

1. We suggested that Jan analyze what part of this situation was causing a problem. Is the goal she wants clear and the first step nebulous, or vice versa? When she performed this first step in reasoning, she discovered that her goal was clear: She wanted to make her son proud and to help other young people in the community. Thus by **STOPping to reason** and using the first P of **PSP**, she could easily identify which strategy to use: **backward reasoning**.

2a. When Jan **wrote her goal** at the top of **Thinking Tool K** and began **backward reasoning**, she realized that the step right before achieving it would be to say things in front of the group that were important and helpful.

   Continuing to reason backward, she wrote that in order to do that, she would read about the successes and failures of others in her field. Because she was an entrepreneur, she could list four autobiographies she wanted to use to prepare. Jan wrote down the four titles and left that minute to go to the library.

   On her way, she continued her backward reasoning and established that she would need to read these books for 15 minutes every day. Because her schedule was tight, she would use the time she normally spent reading the morning paper on these books for the next four weeks.

2b. Then Jan continued her backward reasoning to the week before the speech. She blocked out one hour each evening of that week to write her speech and rehearse it before the mirror. This schedule was a form of **bracketing** — a strategy to keep her from worrying about the speech during the day, so that it would not interfere with her work.

3. The last thing Jan did before calling the principal to accept was to **analyze her talents** and prepare a way to overcome her fear of embarrassing her son and employees. First, she knew one of her best talents was preparing surprises for

others. Therefore, she decided that if she ever received a question from the audience that she couldn't answer, she would use a saying that would make her son proud. The saying would make sense to a wider audience, but had a special private meaning for her and her son.

Also, she used **Proactive Repair** to think of a response to make her employees proud. This was to compliment the person from the audience for asking such a good question, then tell the audience that as she reflected on the answer she would like to take this brief moment to tell the audience how grateful she was to each employee (calling them by name) for the talents they gave and the successes they created. By this time, she was certain, she would have the time to think of an effective answer for the difficult question. As Jan wrote this problem-solving strategy, her **spirits rose**, and she **committed** to giving the best speech possible.

4. Jan knew that one of her talents was to *be the first to speak up* in a small group, and that doing so would decrease her nervousness. She used this **self-knowledge** to reduce her fear of failure: She called the principal and asked if she could be the first person to speak on the panel. The principal readily agreed, and Jan left her desk to tell her son the good news. She couldn't wait to begin reading her new books and preparing to give the best presentation possible!

SITUATION 3 (PERSONAL CHANGE): MORTIMER

In your job, you and Mortimer are viewed as a team. It is up to both of you to perform tasks as a unit. Mortimer is usually late to work, takes longer than his allotted time for lunch, and frequently leaves the job to make telephone calls or to talk with co-workers. You have informally tried to discuss your concerns about his failure to carry his part of the load. Each time, Mortimer has changed his behavior for a while and then reverted back to his former errant ways. You are tired of this seemingly endless litany of irritating performances on his part, and you seek to solve these problems on a long-term basis.

In order to make an effective change, you decide that you will formulate three different strategies and give Mortimer his choice as to which ones the two of you will employ to eliminate these behaviors permanently. Please identify the three strategies you would use. After doing so, rank them in the order which you believe most people would select, and share the three strategies individually with another co-worker. Do not tell them your order of preference. Ask them to describe why they ranked the strategies as they did. The strategies we recommend will be listed after you complete your list.

What strategies will you propose to use?

_____

_____

_____

_____

_____

_____

_____

_____

Based on the information presented, what solution do you think you might reach?

_____

_____

_____

_____

_____

_____

_____

_____

These are the strategies we would recommend you use in your difficulty with Mortimer.

1. Probing for the best pattern (PSP)
2. Using the backward reasoning strategy (PSP)
3. Proactively telling the upside and downside (PSP)

Specifically, by using **Thinking Tool I, Solving Problems Involving Other People by Probing for the Best Interaction** (p. 124), you can discern specific positive and negative spects of the working relationship more objectively. We recommend **backward reasoning** because your ultimate goal is very clear, yet how to begin to reach it is not. Once you complete **Thinking Tool K, Backward Reasoning Steps** (p. 133), you will be ready to **describe the upsides and downsides** of the change you propose that you and Mortimer begin tomorrow, as well as the ultimate goal.

Because you do not know Mortimer's side of the situation, or conditions about your working style that he might prefer to change, you cannot unilaterally state the exact action that will be best for both of you. You do know that merely altering small aspects of tasks has made enormous differences in your life in the past, and that you are not going to give in or give up but to **ante up.** Therefore, the only situation you are willing to agree upon is one in which both of you will benefit.

Before you move on to the next chapter, we want you to take a separate sheet of paper and apply **power thinking** strategies to a difficulty in your own personal life. We encourage you to begin by writing about the difficulty itself. *Do not be afraid to write honestly about the largest problem you are currently facing.* If you have not already done so, cut out the **Thinking Aid** notecards from the back of the book at this time, and place them in front of you as you write. These reminders of the **power thinking** strategies for decision making, problem solving, and personal change will help you as you think about your dilemma.

CHAPTER 9
Home and Family Applications

In Chapter 7, we demonstrated the application of **power thinking** techniques to real-life professional situations. In the same manner, we now present three examples of challenges you might encounter in your home and family life. For two problems, we first present the scenario. Then we set out the course of our thinking as we apply the **power thinking** strategies we have been describing. These will illustrate how we think through the problem situation to arrive at a decision for action. If you desire, you can work through your course of thinking and compare the strategies you would have used in each situation to our thinking course. The third situation is presented for you to work out yourself. Our suggestions appear at the end of the chapter.

SITUATION 1 (DECISION MAKING): TED

Ted has worked for several years as an editor. The books for which he has had major responsibility have made his company an inordinate amount of money. Ted has watched several former editors begin their own publishing companies, make a great deal of money, and derive a great deal of satisfaction from the endeavor.

To do this himself will mean leaving the company which he

has served thirteen years, which has treated him well, and for which he has enjoyed working. (Loyalty is one of Ted's values.) It will mean using all of the family's savings, which he initially intended for his retirement, as well as assuming a small loan. He also knows he will derive no income from the company for the first several months because it will have no books to sell. He wants to make a decision. Ted realizes that starting a company will be the realization of a lifetime dream for him, but he is worried that he will place his family's present and future well-being in jeopardy.

✍ What strategies should Ted use to assess whether to leave his present job and begin his own company? (Refer to the strategies for decision making at the beginning of Chapter 4.)

_____

_____

_____

_____

_____

_____

_____

_____

_____

_____

_____

_____

_____

✍ Based on the information presented, what decision do you think Ted should reach?

_____

The strategies we recommended to Ted were as follows.

1. Ted **STOP**ped to reason and did a **DOUBLE THINK** — in a rather creative way, since Ted is a very innovative person. What he did was to picture himself at two different retirement parties at age 65: one from his current employer, and one from his own company. At each party, he imagined himself in another room listening to comments made by the people who were his co-workers all these years — of whom some admired him, some disliked him, and some were indifferent to him. **Figure 9-1** (below) shows Ted's list of all the comments he imagined these people making.

2. Ted then completed **Thinking Tool E**, the **Weighted Characteristics Test**. **Figure 9-2** (on the next page) shows the results of his **CAUTION**ed reasoning.

3. Next, Ted reviewed the **Excuses List** in **Thinking Tool F** (p. 87). He wrote a powerful alternative for every excuse he

---

FIGURE 9-1

Party at my Current Employer

1. "He made so much money for the company that we all got big raises as a result!"

2. "We'll miss him, but now at least there's room at the top for one of us to be promoted — he's been here for more than 30 years!"

3. "I didn't know him well."

4. "That one idea he had, plus the weight of this large publishing company's name, revolutionized the field."

Party at My Own Company

1. "Because of him, we all will live fulfilled lives because he was so generous with profit sharing and benefits."

2. "Who can possibly fill his shoes?"

3. "Everyone knew him well."

4. "Each one of the 25 books we published made the best-seller list."

FIGURE 9-2
TED'S WEIGHTED CHARACTERISTICS TEST (COMPLETED)

STAY		LEAVE	
1. Know job well, am successful, and gain personal satisfaction from it	3	1. No job security or income for at least a year	1
2. Enjoy recognition of my success from others	4	2. Do not want to place my family at risk, so I can afford one year	6
3. Value the loyalty I've extended this company	5	3. Realize a lifelong dream	12
4. Steady income	2	4. My wife thinks I should go for it if that's what I want	11
5. Bored	9	5. I can be my own boss	8
6. No chance for advancement; I am as high as I can go in this company	7	6. At least I will have tried, even if I fail after my one year's allotment and what I do next is not as lucrative	10
TOTAL	**30**	**TOTAL**	**48**

was giving himself — to stay as well as to leave.

4. Ted analyzed his **ability to say yes and no** to both options and how each decision would affect his **self-esteem**. In doing this, he realized that once he made his decision, he would have no problem committing to either one, as he was really in a win-win situation with many positives on both sides.

5. Thus, Ted decided to allow himself the time his insight needed to commit. After several days of actively considering his options, he realized that his **good indicators** were all coming from the idea of starting his own company.

Based on his results from the use of all these strategies, Ted decided to start his own company. We want to emphasize that you might not make the same decision in a parallel situation, since you are a different person from Ted. If you use **power thinking** to reach your decision, it will be the best one for you, based on all the variables you know at the time.

SITUATION 2 (PROBLEM SOLVING): SUZANNE

Suzanne is 54 years old. She and her husband, a very successful attorney, are happily married and have three children. The youngest has graduated from college and the other two live out of state. Suzanne is depressed, bored, and despondent. She finds her days to be carbon copies of each other. Frequently at the end of the day she feels she has accomplished nothing. She believes she is too old to try something new. Her friends tell her she should begin selling her decorative crafts, but she doesn't believe they are good enough to sell.

Imagine that you are Suzanne's spouse. You love her and realize full well that she is going through this period of unhappiness. You and she agree that this weekend you will put together a plan of action to turn around this malaise she is experiencing.

What strategies do you use?

_____

_____

_____

_____

_____

_____

_____

_____

_____

_____

_____

_____

_____

_____

_____

_____

_____

_____

_____

_____

_____

Based on the information presented, what should Suzanne do?

_____

_____

_____

_____

This was Suzanne's course of **power thinking**:

1. Suzanne used **Thinking Tool H** at the beginning of Chapter 5 (pp. 117–120) to **analyze her beliefs about success and failure**. As she answered each of the statements, she realized that one of the reasons she was so depressed was that she could not remember a single time in her life when she had really judged herself to be successful. "Oh!" she thought. "That's the real problem."

2. She couldn't remember all the problem solving strategies, so she reread Chapter 5. Doing so helped her realize that she should use a **matrix** to analyze her responses to the

potential pros and cons of the craft business and see how she could use her talents to create a successful product. The matrix Suzanne made appears on the next page.

3. Suzanne then reviewed the strategies for **analyzing her most appropriate pace of change**. This analysis showed her that her **good indicators** rose when she outlined a six-month plan (as opposed to a three-month or a one-year plan) for identifying her customer base and plant location.

4. Finally, she realized that to actualize her six-month plan, she would have to **ADAPT** the ideas in her matrix. She established deadlines for building a clientele, restricting her efforts to friends and relatives for the first six months and taking her craft business to the county fair in the second six months. In this way, she could avoid the stress of time pressure that she had felt so often in the past.

SITUATION 3 (PERSONAL CHANGE): YOU

At seminars we have conducted in the past, our participants found it very helpful to actually place themselves in the following hypothetical situation. Doing so enabled them to learn how they responded to stressful change situations *before* they used **power thinking** to truly make a change in their lives. When our participants finish, we have them share their results and realize how powerful the change would be for each person.

Pretend that your spouse was fired. He or she has made several unsuccessful attempts to find a job and feels discouraged. What strategies do you recommend to help your spouse get back on track professionally?

_____

_____

_____

_____

FIGURE 9-2: SUZANNE'S MATRIX (COMPLETED)

Interacting Factors		Craft Industry Pitfalls In the Past that I'll Overcome			
		Too Cutesy	Too Faddish, Not Permanent	Off An Assembly Line/ Not Personal	Too Seasonal
M Y **T A L E N T S**	Artistic	Will add masculine as well as feminine aspects	Will make things of permanent utility to a house	Will personalize with customers' names in calligraphy	Will use 4 different versions to have one for each season
	Wood Carving	Will make a strong background base	Hooks will be permanent and easy to use	Customer can select personalized decorations	Background will be versatile - a circle instead of a Christmas tree
	Sewing	[Takes too long and I don't enjoy this so I will glue instead of sewing]			
	Floral Arranging	Can make the most realistic silk flowers ever!	I've done a survey of which flowers people like best	Will guarantee no two wreaths are ever the same	Customer can select types & color schemes they desire

_____

_____

_____

_____

_____

_____

_____

_____

_____

_____

_____

_____

_____

✍ What is the ultimate plan of action?

_____

_____

_____

_____

_____

_____

_____

After answering both questions, turn the page to read the strategies used most frequently in our seminars to respond to this situation. Doing so will enable you to assess how well you know these strategies.

We recommend:

1. Practicing **CAP**ped speech prior to interviews.

2. Analyzing past **flow experiences.**

3. Analyzing **talents, needs, and motivations.**

4. **Bracketing** and internal problem solving space.

5. Seeking good advice and **going to the person in charge.**

6. **PSP.**

7. **Vision versus Daydreams.**

8. **Anteing up** instead of getting out or giving in to something that the spouse does not want to do.

9. Applying **ADAPT** creativity strategies.

Now, we encourage you to take a separate sheet of paper and apply **power thinking** strategies to a difficulty in your home relations. Doing this will help you change the difficulty more rapidly.

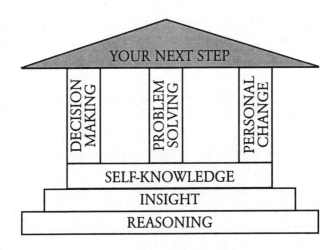

DECISION MAKING · PROBLEM SOLVING · PERSONAL CHANGE

SELF-KNOWLEDGE

INSIGHT

REASONING

YOUR NEXT STEP

CHAPTER 10
Your Next Step

After his junior year at the University of Pittsburgh, Dan Marino was regarded by most football experts as the best quarterback in college football. It was predicted he would be one of the first players, if not *the* first, to be selected in the next National Football League (NFL) draft at the end of the following year.

Unfortunately, several unanticipated events occurred before the NFL draft day arrived. For one thing, the University of Pittsburgh team didn't challenge for the national championship as they were expected to do. They suffered a few unanticipated losses and were lackluster in several of their wins. Dan's performance was disappointing at times. Yes, he threw many completed passes, and for lots of yardage, but he also was plagued by numerous interceptions and incomplete passes in key instances. Nor were Dan's chances in the NFL draft helped by his final game as a collegian, a Cotton Bowl loss by Pittsburgh to Southern Methodist University.

On NFL draft day, there was a great deal of conjecture as to when Dan would be selected and by which team. The draft began, and as teams selected players, Dan's name wasn't among them. In fact, several quarterbacks were chosen before Dan. Finally, it came time for his hometown professional football team, the Pittsburgh Steelers, to make its selection. It was known they were in dire need of a quarterback, and since they had seen him perform on so many occasions, most sports commentators thought the Steelers were certain to select Dan. But they didn't; they chose another collegian instead. Finally, Dan Marino was selected by the Miami Dolphins.

To anyone familiar with professional football, the career of Dan Marino is well known. He has become not just a superstar for the Dolphins, but one of the NFL's all-time greatest players. His statistics — completed passes, total passing yardage, touchdown passes, games his team won with him at quarterback, etc. — are monumental. Above all, Dan Marino has been a huge part of the Dolphins winning football games. He is a fiery competitor who simply refuses to believe his team is capable of losing a football game. When his career is over, Dan Marino will be selected for the National Football League's Hall of Fame, a honor bestowed only on the very finest football players to ever play the game.

We relate the Dan Marino story to you because in some respects, the possibilities in your future parallel the possibilities Dan Marino faced following the NFL draft. Dan could have continued to throw incomplete passes and interceptions as a professional. He would have justified the so-called experts' estimation of him. Instead, Dan used the opportunity to "begin a new page" in his career. He learned new ways of performing as a quarterback, and he developed additional confidence in his ability to be a winner.

At this juncture, you are faced with decisions similar to those confronting Dan Marino after the NFL draft. You have just finished reading a book in which we presented you with numerous new ways to perform in the world of work and in your personal life. You could dismiss the ideas as impractical or too time-consuming. Or you could cite external factors (they won't work at my company, my boss would fire me if I did them, etc.) as reasons for not implementing them into your *modus operandi*. Or you could procrastinate. You could say, for example, you intend to implement them "when things aren't quite so busy in my life."

You have another recourse available to you. Just as Dan Marino "began a new page" in his life, you now have the same opportunity. The strategies presented in this book promote success. We recognize their implementation will mean change in your life. We also know that for many people, change is uncomfortable. It means forsaking long-established modes of behavior as well as some facets of your personality that have brought you a certain degree of past success.

Why change, then? We contend that the strategies in this book will enhance you not only personally but also professionally. We believe you will become happier, more confident, and more satisfied with yourself and your life. In the world of work, we think you will derive not only more enjoyment from your position but also will be appreciably more successful in it.

Dan Marino went from being a very good college quarterback to being a future NFL Hall of Fame ballplayer. You are confronted with a very clear choice — do you want to continue to perform at the same level as you did last year, last month, and last week, or do you want to perform much better? If you respond affirmatively to the latter, please read on.

Now that you have made a commitment to change past behaviors, you are ready to begin to make changes occur. Your first step should be the development of a plan of action.

On subsequent pages, you will find a device that will help you to develop a plan of action that is appropriate for *you*. It contains all the strategies that have been presented to you in prior chapters. The strategies are shown in the sequence they appeared in this book. For example in Chapter 1, we discussed:

Reasoning	Insight	Self-Knowledge
STOP: read/reflect/write	Break Away	Talents/Needs/Motives
CAUTION: listen/ask questions	High Spirits	Analyze Beliefs
GO: Speech CAPped	Create Flow	Strong Self-Concept

In addition to listing the book's content, we also have provisions for implementation. We want you to consider which strategies you *now* feel can enrich and add power to your thinking processes. The procedure is a relatively simple one. First, we ask that you identify those strategies you used before you read this book and that you plan to continue to use. Next, we ask that you select those strategies that you hadn't used in the past, but which you plan to make an integral part of your behavior. While we cannot say with certainty how many new items should be on your intended plan of action, we have found that for most individuals five seems to be an optimal number. Finally, we ask that you monitor your progress in realizing your plan's ingredients.

It has been our experience that a three-month plan of action is usually most appropriate. Thus, if you select strategy X as one which you plan to initiate, we ask that you monitor its use at least monthly for three months. Check your use every three months thereafter. When you have used it regularly and successfully for about a year, it's relatively safe to assume that you have internalized the strategy and that it is now part of you. Even after that year has passed, you will find rereading the chapter helpful to clarify points that may have confused you before. You will continue to add new dimensions to your **power thinking**. Don't be discouraged if you at first cannot use the strategies as readily as we have explained them. There is a long learning curve for some of this material!

As strategies become a permanent part of you, it will be appropriate to consider adding new ones to your repertoire. We suggest that each year, you take stock of yourself and see which strategies are now part of you as well as which ones you'd like to devote attention to in the months ahead. Again, using the same scenario, choose no more than five strategies to focus on during any given period. Don't try to conquer the whole world at one time! If you overburden yourself, you set yourself up for discouragement and ultimately sabotage your own **power thinking**.

Above all, do not think of the process of adding and moving in a rigid way. It is meant to be fluid, and as you change, so too should the strategies you are implementing. For example, after successfully making strategy Y a part of you, you may now feel a need for strategy Z. If you think such a strategy needs to be acquired, then by all means pursue it. These strategies are no longer our strategies but our resources available to *you* as you seek to improve yourself and your performance.

YOUR PLAN OF ACTION

☞ **Directions:** Place a check mark (✓) next to any strategy you have used in the past, and a plus sign (+) beside those strategies you plan to utilize in the next 3 months.

The first column is for those items you are currently using which you plan to continue, as well as those you will initiate in the next 3 months. Repeat the process again 3 months from now, placing check marks and pluses in the second column. Use the third column 3 months after that, and so on. (Eight columns have been provided for you, but once all eight have been completed, feel free to add additional, new columns to monitor your subsequent activities).

Do not change the designation of an item from a plus to a check mark until you feel it is ingrained in your behavior. For most individuals, we have found this will take from 6 months to one year to occur.

What You Can Expect: A Cautionary Note

Now, you begin your own journey to develop your **power thinking**. As we told you in the Introduction, it can be an immensely fruitful journey, but it will not be an easy one. We want to caution you here *not to become discouraged early in the process*. Such disappointment may cause you to lose heart and give up. That is why we reiterate now the difficulty of the task you are embarking upon.

You may think that once you have read this book and thought about what you have learned, you can instantly apply the principles and procedures we have described and they will work perfectly for you. However, the thinking processes you now use were acquired over the course of a lifetime! They have worked for you,

PERSONAL PLAN OF ACTION			Assessment Dates											
REASONING														
STOP: read/ reflect/ write	DOUBLE THINK													
	P = PROBING FOR BEST PATTERN													
	ENTRAPMENT / COST OF LOST OPPORTUNITY													
CAUTION: listen/ ask questions	WEIGHTED CHARACTERISTICS TEST													
	S = SELECT STRATEGY													
	WHAT ABOUT PRESENT BRINGS PLEASURE?													
GO: CAPped Speech	REPLACE EXCUSES WITH EXPLANATIONS													
	P = PROACTIVELY													
	GO TO PERSON IN CHARGE													
INSIGHT														
Break Away	COMMIT													
	INTERNAL PROBLEM-SOLVING SPACE													

SELF-KNOWLEDGE

High Spirits	AWAIT GOOD INDICATORS
	UP INSTEAD OF OUT OR IN
	DEPRESSION
Create Flow	PROACTIVE REPAIR
	VISION VS. DAYDREAMS
	PACE OF CHANGE
Talents/ Needs/ Motives	CONQUER HUMAN NATURE
	GOOD ADVICE
	CHANGE SELF, NOT OTHERS
Analyze Beliefs	BELIEFS ABOUT SAYING YES AND NO
	BELIEFS ABOUT SUCCESS AND FAILURE
	NEGATIVE PATTERNS
Strong Self-Concept	MONITOR YOUR SELF-RESPECT
	SELF-RESILIENCY
	CREATIVITY

and you have relied on them. Now you have decided to change the approaches you have used or add new ones. Merely contemplating these changes will not make them happen! It is *hard work* to re-structure the thinking habits of a lifetime. It takes considerable time, discipline, and conscious effort. That is why we have included the **Thinking Aid** graphics at the end of the book. They are intended to support your efforts by serving as concrete reminders of the strategies you wish to incorporate.

You may need to work your way through this book several times before the processes make complete sense to you. This feeling does not mean that our lessons are unsound, or that you are unable to acquire the skills. With diligence and practice, you *will* internalize the nuances of the steps, so that they converge into a natural and more automatic script. (Even after you reach that level of proficiency, you should still revisit the book occasionally — for reference on a particular step, as a general refresher, or to add new elements of **power thinking** to your repertoire.) You have to develop a sense of how slowly your own thought process undergoes change. Pay attention to the rate of success of your initial efforts. This will help you gain a sense of the work which real and lasting change involves.

Several times throughout the book, we remind you of the importance of selecting *small steps*. When you take on these changes in small chunks, you can focus on one specific change at a time you want to implement, and establish it firmly in your thinking habits. If you choose too large a goal, you may be discouraged when it doesn't all come together as easily as you expected. Take it easy; take it slow — but take it with determination, and **power thinking** is within your grasp!

In the office of one of our friends who is a great leader, there is a sign that says: "Lead, follow, or get out of the way." When questioned about it, he responded that there are instances when he must be out front on a particular issue. In other instances, a subordinate must be in that situation and it is his responsibility to follow that person's directions. There are also times when he must "get out of the way" so that others may be better able to sift and winnow through a task and learn from it.

It is now time for us to get out of *your* way as you begin to sift and winnow your way through what you've learned in this book and to determine what strategies you'll employ in the future. We began this book by asking you why you wanted to read it, and what you hoped we would tell you in it. Please return to page xviii and read what you wrote there.

✍ Has reading and thinking about the content of this book changed what you would write now? How?

_____

_____

_____

_____

It was our goal in writing this book to provide strategies in which you can begin to find this answer for yourself. We hope the days ahead bring you personal happiness and professional success. We have enjoyed being with you.

About the Authors

DR. JOHN N. MANGIERI, Director of the Institute for Effective Management in Cambridge, Massachusetts, received his Ph.D. from the University of Pittsburgh. Dr. Mangieri has served on the faculty of Ohio University, the University of South Carolina, and Texas Christian University. He has also held a variety of administrative positions, including university president.

Dr. Mangieri, a Fulbright scholar, is the author or co-author of 87 professional articles and 12 books. Among these are *Creating Powerful Thinking in Teachers and Students* (Harcourt Brace) and *Reason to Read: Thinking Strategies for Life Through Literature*, Vols. 1–3 (Addison-Wesley).

DR. CATHY COLLINS BLOCK, Professor of Education at Texas Christian University, received her Ph.D. from the University of Wisconsin—Madison. She has taught at Southern Illinois University—Carbondale, served on the staff of the Wisconsin Research and Development Center for Cognitive Development, and taught kindergarten through high school-aged students in private and public schools. She has directed five research projects in thinking development and served as Chairperson of the National Commission to Infuse Thinking Development into the Curriculum (Washington, DC, 1991–92) and Director of the Texas Network of Thinking Schools (1989–93).

Dr. Block has written more than 50 articles and several books, including co-editing *Creating Powerful Thinking in Teachers and Students* (Harcourt Brace) and *Teaching Thinking: An Agenda for the 21st Century* (Erlbaum), authoring *Teaching the Language Arts: Developing Thinking Through Student-Centered Instruction* (Allyn & Bacon), and co-authoring *Reason to Read: Thinking Strategies for Life through Literature*, Vols. 1–3 (Addison-Wesley).

APPENDIX
Easy-to-Reference Thinking Aids

Cut out the Thinking Aid notecard for each strategy you wish to acquire. Use it as a reminder to incorporate the strategy into your mental routine. See the Introduction for suggestions on the use of these notecards.

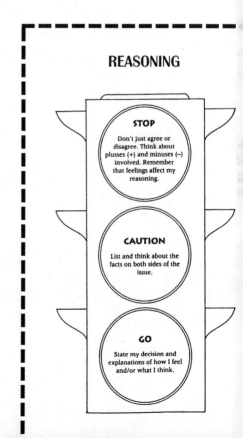

REASONING

STOP

Don't just agree or disagree. Think about plusses (+) and minuses (–) involved. Remember that feelings affect my reasoning.

CAUTION

List and think about the facts on both sides of the issue.

GO

State my decision and explanations of how I feel and/or what I think.

THINKING AID 1
PAGE 3

ASK QUESTIONS TO CLARIFY

ASK

OFTEN

INSIGHT

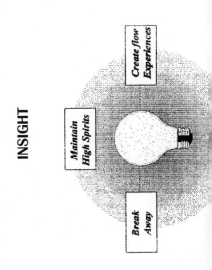

- Maintain High Spirits
- Create flow Experiences
- Break Away

THE EMOTIONAL SCALE

6. Faith, Hope, Enthusiasm
5. Love
3. Fear
2. Hurt
1. Anger

KEYS TO SELF-KNOWLEDGE

KEEP YOUR SPIRITS HIGH

Keep Score

SELF-MOTIVATION, PASSION, DRIVE, AND HOPE

- BELIEFS
- SELF-CONCEPTS
- TALENTS, MOTIVATION NEEDS
- PERSONAL ANALYSIS

THINKING AID 3
PAGE 27

Power Thinking for Success!
© 1996

THINKING AID 2
PAGE 13

Power Thinking for Success!
© 1996

THINKING AID 5
PAGE 41

Power Thinking for Success!
© 1996

THINKING AID 4
PAGE 32

Power Thinking for Success!
© 1996

EVALUATE YOUR BELIEFS

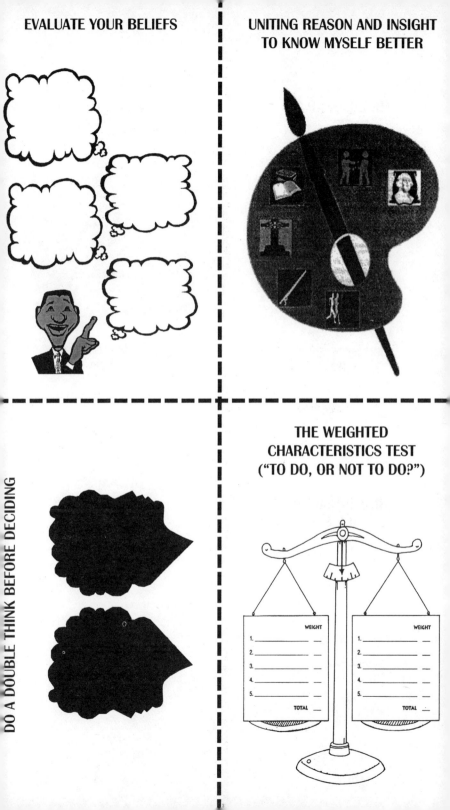

UNITING REASON AND INSIGHT TO KNOW MYSELF BETTER

DO A DOUBLE THINK BEFORE DECIDING

THE WEIGHTED CHARACTERISTICS TEST ("TO DO, OR NOT TO DO?")

WEIGHT

1. _____
2. _____
3. _____
4. _____
5. _____

TOTAL ____

WEIGHT

1. _____
2. _____
3. _____
4. _____
5. _____

TOTAL ____

**THINKING AID 7
PAGE 71**

**THINKING AID 6
PAGE 57**

**THINKING AID 9
PAGE 81**

**THINKING AID 8
PAGE 74**

WINNERS DO NOT GIVE OR USE EXCUSES!

COMMITMENT COUNTERACTS INDECISION

OVERCOMING HUMAN NATURE REDUCES INDECISIVENESS

SAY "NO" EFFECTIVELY

**THINKING AID 11
PAGE 92**

Power Thinking for Success!
© 1996

**THINKING AID 10
PAGE 88**

Power Thinking for Success!
© 1996

**THINKING AID 13
PAGE 109**

Power Thinking for Success!
© 1996

**THINKING AID 12
PAGE 102**

Power Thinking for Success!
© 1996

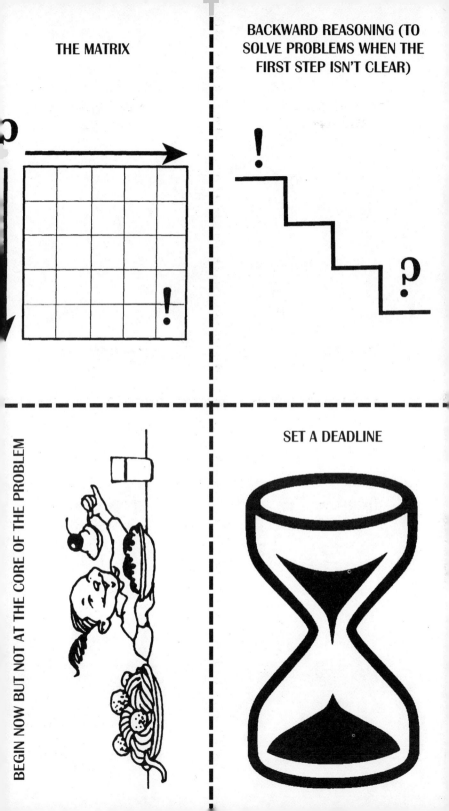

THE MATRIX

BACKWARD REASONING (TO SOLVE PROBLEMS WHEN THE FIRST STEP ISN'T CLEAR)

BEGIN NOW BUT NOT AT THE CORE OF THE PROBLEM

SET A DEADLINE

THINKING AID 15
PAGE 132

Power Thinking for Success!
© 1996

THINKING AID 14
PAGE 127

Power Thinking for Success!
© 1996

THINKING AID 17
PAGE 138

Power Thinking for Success!
© 1996

THINKING AID 16
PAGE 135

Power Thinking for Success!
© 1996

MAKE AN ASSEMBLY LINE

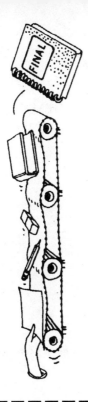

CHANNEL SOLUTIONS INTO YOUR TALENT AREAS

**BRACKETING TO MAINTAIN
PERSPECTIVE AND POWER
THINKING TOWARD
PRODUCTIVE GAINS**

ANTE UP INSTEAD OF GETTING OUT OR GIVING IN

THINKING AID 19
PAGE 143

THINKING AID 18
PAGE 141

THINKING AID 21
PAGE 149

THINKING AID 20
PAGE 147

VISION VS. DAYDREAMS

FOUR TYPES OF CHANGE = FOUR TYPES OF RISK

...L PEOPLE THE DOWNSIDES AND UPSIDES TO
POTENTIAL CHANGES

"ADAPT" CREATIVELY TO CHANGE MORE EFFECTIVELY

THINKING AID 23
PAGE 162

THINKING AID 22
PAGE 151

THINKING AID 25
PAGE 182

THINKING AID 24
PAGE 174